The Executive Guide to
Six Sigma Call Centers

By James C. Abbott

Robert
Houston
Smith
Publishers

Robert Houston Smith Publishers
PO Box 25156
Greenville, SC 29616
864-627-1278 (telephone)
864-297-8624 (facsimile)
www.RHSPublishers.com
books@RHSPublishers.com

ISBN: 978-1-887-355-11-7

© 2008 by Abbott Associates Incorporated

Printed in the United States of America

Dedication:

I want to acknowledge two people whose contributions have been vital. Kelly Boland is a skilled writer and professional editor. She has provided critical assistance in this and other books by providing expert organization, planning, and editing. Ron Parker is a brilliant practitioner of mathematics and science. He has provided a wonderful sounding board for new ideas.

To both of you, my deepest appreciation and thanks for all your hard work.

James C Abbott

Table of Contents

Introduction:

Six Sigma in the Call Center World

As we start our discussion of a six sigma call center design, clarity of purpose is essential. This clear purpose is our call center vision. A clear vision of what our call center is about will provide the insight as to when we are successful. A clear policy outlining our mission is critical to designing the center

Six sigma is having a service or making a product that is virtually flawless each and every time. More details will come about why six, what exactly a sigma is, and why sigma is important, but this simple definition will get us started.

The call center manager's goal is to continually improve while at the same time making his customers happy. This goal is a never-ending journey for improvement. What is acceptable or terrific today will be considered terrible tomorrow.

Every company values their customers. Customers are the source of their revenue. Many times the company does not act as if they value their customer because they waste their customers' time by making them wait on the phone or computer. If companies paid their customers a cost per minute for each time they made them wait, we might view things very differently. What if the customer charged us $5, or $10, or $20 per hour for waiting? We might rethink some of our strategies. We might find a disconnect between our policy and our strategies.

Many call center managers are one-dimensional and that leads to a trouble zone. For example, by focusing on wait time and totally ignoring cost, we risk escalating our cost to an unreasonable level as we try to fix wait-time problems by simply throwing money at them. To help us avoid this kind of trouble zone, we will develop a balanced goal to use throughout this book as a means of describing our objective for call center improvement. This balanced goal must give equal weight and importance to wait time, cost, and performance. The six sigma mission is achieving each simultaneously. For years manufacturing has used six sigma to reduce variability. Now, as our economy moves more and more into the service sector, the concept of six sigma must be applied there.

Introduction

Many use the term six sigma for quality, and our definition of quality is quite broad. **Quality** means meeting or exceeding the customer's perceived expectations and requirements while reducing cost and providing the product to the customer when he wants it. Thus, our goal.

The three components we've discussed — performance, cost, and time-- define quality. Quality gives us a total definition. This definition is most commonly used in manufacturing. In call centers, rather than quality, a better choice of words is value. Our principle concern is to always strive to provide the best value to the customer. The key word to describe the three dimensions of quality is **value**.

We can add value throughout the organization. Shareholders' value is increased by more effective operations that reduce the cost. Customer value is increased by reducing wait time and giving better service through excellent performance. These customer value increases will also lead to increased revenue thereby increasing shareholder value. Finally, associates' value increases through better work environment and realistic expectations.

A six sigma design or program provides value but much more. Change is the one constant that we can really count on in this 21st century. This change is moving at a lightning speed. New products and services are the direct result of this change, and they too are coming at lightning speed.

With a six sigma design in your center, these new products and services can seamlessly and easily blend into the fold for rapid deployment. We can quickly accomplish adding new product and services.

The following are more possibilities. We can radically optimize our facility. We have many options for optimally redeploying our assets. We can increase our agents' value through career migrations, career paths, better workplace, and rapid training. These will reduce our agent attrition.

In a traditional call center everybody has to be knowledgeable on the all products and services both old and new. All the new people must be trained on all the old products and services and then also trained on the new products and services. In this book, we learn about six sigma segmentation to avoid the traditional approach's problems with changing and the addition of new products. This segmentation can be used in an approach called express lanes, which will be covered throughout this book.

In the chapter on *Optimizing a Sigma Design* we will see what a large difference in the number of required hours a sigma-designed center has versus one with no thought given to sigma. The sigma center allows you to reduce the number of required hours and, by managing variability, give a better customer experience.

In a traditional center where everyone is doing everything, we can set only one utilization target because all the calls, the agents, and the utilizations are pooled. In a sigma designed center, in addition to minimizing hours, we can set utilizations for each express lane based on the lane-specific drivers so that we refine our center even more.

In a center where everyone is doing everything, the only adjustment is adding or removing people. In a sigma-designed center a supervisor or manager can move resources from one express lane to another. Each express lane can have utilization set for the specifics of the lane.

In a sigma design, an agent's training is a step at a time. Just in time training allows the agent to be trained on the roles and responsibilities the agent is going to be immediately working on.

In a sigma design an agent can migrate through the center increasing their knowledge in a stepped fashion. As each step is accomplished, the agent's knowledge increases. The agent's self worth will grow and the agent's value to the company will grow. This gives a way for us to keep a steady stream of increasingly competent people moving through the center.

As our agent's expertise grows, the center can act as a spawning ground for other parts of the company. The sigma-designed center gives the agents a migration path through the center and a career path out of the center.

The sigma-designed center will allow us to reduce cost but still give the customer a great experience. This balanced view of the center will allow us to contribute to increasing the value of the company.

Call centers have been around since 1900, when telephone operators would connect you to the party that you were trying to reach. Since those early beginnings, call centers have radically changed.

Introduction

Over a century later the call center is the storefront for the enterprise. Call centers are classified into five types. These call center types are routing, notification, call management, processing, and content dissemination. The routing call center transfers the caller to the correct party. The notification center notifies the receiver of the call and any message. Call management manages the call from receipt to resolution. Call management tracks and documents every step that is done to the request. Processing is where the service acts on the request. The businesses using this service include sales, order taking, billing, computer setup, etc. Content dissemination gives advice and shares information via any medium (phone, fax, web, email, etc.)

The modern call center and understanding the differing roles of call centers has a profound impact on why six sigma designs are crucial.

Our six sigma call center design is guided by the answer to three questions: Why, What, and How. *Why* is answered by science and education. *What* is answered by an operational philosophy, process management principles, and engineering. *How* is answered with processes, metrics, and technology. This book will show you their importance. Then you will see how to apply them in your call center and help desk.

This book will explain why a sigma design in a call center and help desk is critical.

What is a Sigma?

20th Century Centers

Twenty-first century call centers have radically changed from their beginnings in the early 1900s. Through most of the 20th century call centers and help desks were simply routing centers. Using averages worked well because all calls were about the same. Let's first explore how and why this technique worked so well for decades.

Our first study will revolve around a common problem. We will analyze the call volume, over time, for a call center. The table below shows the call volume for the years 2000, 2001, 2002, and part of the year 2003. The information gained from this study will be used to plan the required facilities for the call center.

Call Volume				
	2000	2001	2002	2003
January	2749	4081	4982	3936
February	5405	5004	4299	5024
March	3936	2708	3793	3239
April	2232	2423	1870	
May	1079	1493	1514	
June	1330	2197	1713	
July	2616	2918	1890	
August	2820	2041	1897	
September	2321	2041	1923	
October	1583	1494	1316	
November	1877	1859	1843	
December	3439	3936	2919	

When we were children, we used to play on a seesaw or teeter-totter. One of the main things we tried to do was get the seesaw to balance two people on opposite ends of a board. The spot the board rests on is called the fulcrum.

When both sides weigh equal amounts, the fulcrum is positioned in the center. When one side weighs more than the other, the board will tilt toward the side of the heavier weight. By moving the fulcrum toward the heavier weight, we can find a position where the seesaw will once again balance.

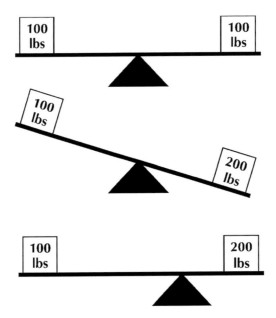

This balance point is critical information in many fields like physics and mechanical engineering. Balance associated with numeric measurements is essential to statistics. The balance point is called **central tendency**.

Monitors of Central Tendency

Since central tendency is critical to understanding numeric measurements, monitors of it must be established. There are several central tendency monitors—average, mode, and median. The typical and most often used monitor of central tendency is average. **Average** is *a point estimate of the measurement of the central tendency of the data*. Average is a statistical tool to monitor the central tendency. It is also referred to as the mean or the arithmetic mean. All the different names — average, mean, and arithmetic mean — are describing the same monitor. Average is the balance point of all the data points giving equal weight to each value.

Average

The average monitors central tendency. Average divides the sum of the measurements by the number of measurements. To compute the average call volume for the year 2000, individual call volume for each of the 12 months is added and then divided by the total number of months (12). The total calls for 2000 is 31,387, which is then divided by 12 to arrive at the average of 2,616 calls per month.

The following chart shows how the average of 2,616 is representing the central tendency of call volume data for 2000.

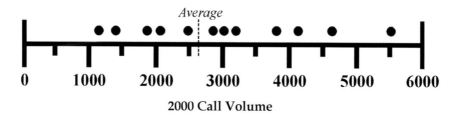

2000 Call Volume

Note how clearly the average shows the center point of call volume. During the 20th century averages served us well, because most of the things that we monitored were the same. In a typical routing call center all the calls were handled the same and most of the calls took about the same length of time. In a 21st century center this trait is not true and average by itself does not paint a clear picture. This does not mean that using averages is wrong or should not be used. The bigger issue is that monitoring central tendency would not suffice by itself. In other words, never use average as a stand-alone measure of a set of values. Central tendency should not be discussed without a companion monitor of variability. Averages can be misleading.

The three sets of data below are intended to demonstrate that simply looking at an average can give an erroneous impression.

The first and third columns under each month are the case numbers. The second and fourth columns show the time to restore for the adjacent case number. The first set of data is January's case number 1, which was restored in 25 minutes. January's case 2 was restored in 27 minutes. Case 3 was restored in 24 minutes. Case 10 from January was restored in 26 minutes. The table below shows the January, February, and March restore times, by case.

Time to Restore in Minutes											
January				February				March			
1	25	9	24	1	25	9	25	1	10	9	35
2	27	10	26	2	25	10	25	2	15	10	15
3	24	11	27	3	25	11	25	3	20	11	40
4	25	12	23	4	25	12	25	4	25	12	35
5	26	13	25	5	25	13	25	5	20	13	30
6	26	14	25	6	25	14	25	6	15	14	25
7	24	15	24	7	25	15	58	7	10	15	30
8	23	16	26	8	2	16	25	8	25	16	35
		17	25			17	25			17	40
Average		25		Average		25		Average		25	

Suppose we are trying to compare the time to restore for outages in an IT organization by month. Notice that all three of the months wind up with exactly the same average of 25 minutes per outage, but all the values of the data set are radically different. The first set of values is relatively close to the average. The second set has two values extremely removed from the other values. The third set has a widely dispersed set of values. The only common link between values is that they all have an average of 25 minutes per outage.

The IT support center might use the 25-minute average to plan by and publish that the system will be restored in this time. The organization might plan based on this and create false impressions. Metrics must provide a clear summary picture of our numbers. Data must be prepared properly to assure that these kinds of prediction mistakes are avoided. We must always get a complete picture of our data. Nothing is wrong with the average, but it shows only part of the picture.

Now let's expand our knowledge and add another component that is needed to complement the average. This component is the amount or magnitude of spread associated with our measurements.

21st Century Centers

In the 21st century, rather than one simple call center type where everyone does the same thing and every call is about the same length, we have five uniquely different call center types. The five types — routing, notification, call management, processing, and content dissemination — require specialized tools, methods, processes, and metrics.

In the early days of the simple call center, the center's largest expenses were far and away telephone service charges. These large and complex phone bills drove management to focus on these telephone charges. Today the science inside the center is more complex because of the many demands from the five different call center types. This requires a conceptual understanding of call center science issues, from express lane determination, to lane balancing, plus the original telephony issues. Metrics play a huge role in the design of an effective call center and the decision-making required to run an optimal call center.

Metrics are the information for running a center. Not having metrics is like an airliner not having gauges like an altimeter. You can fly the plane when the conditions are smooth and clear, but when the plane is in bad weather you are in real trouble. You can have a center with no metrics, but you can only run an effective center when you have the information metrics provides.

With the five types of centers our monitor of central tendency, average, is still important, but it must be complemented with a sigma to track spread — more properly called variability.

Magnitude of Spread

We have seen from the call volume and time to restore examples that an average by itself can be very misleading. This would be like saying that all people who weigh the same amount look the same. One person has a spread up top, and the other has a lower spread. If we were analyzing people's weights, we would want to make sure that we had an additional technique to monitor this spread.

When we are doing analysis, a technique for monitoring spread is required as well. The name for the magnitude of the spread is **variability**. Variability is what sigma is trying to monitor.

Sigma Measures Variability

We need to have a way of distinguishing the difference between the three months from the prior discussion. The means of doing this is called monitoring the variability. Variability, or magnitude of spread, is monitored by a thing called sigma. Sigma is indicated by the Greek letter σ. As the variability or spread increases, the sigma will be larger. Sigma is the value if we knew precisely the magnitude of the spread. Let's start by reviewing several measures of variability, starting with a simple approach. Our first technique for monitoring the variability of the measurements is by viewing the highest and lowest values of the data.

When using minimum and maximum data, two values are always required. This can be simplified by using the distance between the maximum and minimum values. This distance is called the range value. Sometimes the range is abbreviated as R value. **Range** is *a measure of the variability of a set of numbers.* The smaller the range, the lower the variability, or the amount of spread.

Using the call volume data to compute the range for the year 2000, the highest value for the call volume is 5,405 and the lowest value is 1,079. The range for 2000 call volume equals $X_{Max} - X_{Min}$. The values can then be placed in the equation to compute the range. The 2000 range is 4,326 calls. The chart below shows our monthly call volume on a graph along with the average, maximum, minimum, and range values.

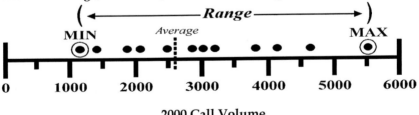

2000 Call Volume

Interpretation and Use of Range

As the range increases, the magnitude of the variability (spread) increases. Should the range be zero, all values are the same and the average is a perfect indicator of each data point. The larger the range, the more variable the data. As the range increases, the average becomes a less precise indicator of the actual values.

The three sets of data in the time to restore chart demand some monitor of variability to clearly depict the different months.

Time to Restore in Minutes											
January				February				March			
1	25	9	24	1	25	9	25	1	10	9	35
2	27	10	26	2	25	10	25	2	15	10	15
3	24	11	27	3	25	11	25	3	20	11	40
4	25	12	23	4	25	12	25	4	25	12	35
5	26	13	25	5	25	13	25	5	20	13	30
6	26	14	25	6	25	14	25	6	15	14	25
7	24	15	24	7	25	15	58	7	10	15	30
8	23	16	26	8	2	16	25	8	25	16	35
		17	25			17	25			17	40
Average			25	Average			25	Average			25
Maximum			27	Maximum			58	Maximum			40
Minimum			23	Minimum			2	Minimum			10
Range			4	Range			56	Range			30

By using range and average together, we can begin to understand the differences in the three sets of data. January has a mean time to restore of 25 minutes and a range of 4 minutes. This drives us to the conclusion that January's outages are all close to the mean. February has a mean time to restore of 25 minutes and a range of 56 minutes. We would conclude that February's outages are very widely spread. March has a mean time to restore of 25 minutes and a range of 30 minutes. We would conclude that March's outages are also widely spread.

Since the range values for both February and March are high, we might conclude that both months have similar restore times. We can see by analyzing the data, however, that the times for February and March are very different. February has two very extreme values with the remaining times all being equal to 25 minutes. All of March's times are different. Therefore, the range value fails us in differentiating between these two months.

We must always get a complete picture of our data. Nothing is wrong with the average, but it only tells part of the story. To add more precision to our study, we must monitor both central tendency (average) and variability together. Neither one can be used without the other.

Properly prepared statistical information can be a wonderful tool for estimates and predictions for all decision-making, including our IT organization plans. Now our IT organization can anticipate restore times because the statistics have painted a more vivid picture that includes both central tendency and variability. Our plans can now be made with reliable and predictable results while avoiding the disaster of exceeding our planned budget.

We now return to our call volume example.

Call Volume				
	2000	2001	2002	2003
January	2749	4081	4982	3936
February	5405	5004	4299	5024
March	3936	2708	3793	3239
April	2232	2423	1870	
May	1079	1493	1514	
June	1330	2197	1713	
July	2616	2918	1890	
August	2820	2041	1897	
September	2321	2041	1923	
October	1583	1494	1316	
November	1877	1859	1843	
December	3439	3936	2919	
Average	2616	2683	2497	4066
Range	4326	3511	3666	1785

The call volume average and range work together to allow us to begin planning our call center needs. The average for 2000 is 2,616 calls with a range of 4,326 calls. A range of this magnitude in relation to its average is quite large. Our conclusion would indicate that large swings from month to month should be anticipated if 2000 is representative of the future.

The year 2001 also has a large range of 3,511 calls in relation to its average of 2,683 calls; this reinforces our conclusion from the analysis of 2000. Similarly, 2002 has a large range of 3,666 calls in relation to the average of 2,497.

Since 2003's call volume is incomplete, no conclusion should be made from the data. To increase our information about the spread of the data, a more advanced method of monitoring variability is required. This improved method should include all of the data.

Standard Deviation Estimates Sigma

In many respects, **standard deviation** is simply a more elaborate range calculation. Thus the method for interpreting standard deviation is similar to the method for interpreting range. As an alternative to a simple range, we could possibly develop a range value for each data point.

To solve the problem of an unmanageable number of range values, we could try to calculate an average range. This idea is great. It allows us to take into account all the data points and give them equal weight.

The standard deviation is abbreviated as S or Std, while variance uses S^2. In many respects, standard deviation is simply a more elaborate range calculation. Thus, the method for interpreting standard deviation is similar to the method for interpreting range.

Interpreting Sigma

As the magnitude of the sigma monitored by standard deviation increases, the variability increases. Should the standard deviation be zero, all values are the same. Thus, average becomes a perfect indicator of all the data with a standard deviation equal to zero. Standard deviations are all positive numbers. As the standard deviation increases, the spread of the data increases.

In the statistical community the symbol sigma, shown as σ, is used to signify a population's variability. The symbol mu, shown as μ, is used to signify a population's central tendency. We can see that standard deviation is a monitor of variability or sigma. Many people interchange the term standard deviation and sigma, because standard deviation is an estimate of variability.

The following table shows our IT support center comparison, adding the standard deviation for each.

Time to Restore in Minutes											
January				February				March			
1	25	9	24	1	25	9	25	1	10	9	35
2	27	10	26	2	25	10	25	2	15	10	15
3	24	11	27	3	25	11	25	3	20	11	40
4	25	12	23	4	25	12	25	4	25	12	35
5	26	13	25	5	25	13	25	5	20	13	30
6	26	14	25	6	25	14	25	6	15	14	25
7	24	15	24	7	25	15	58	7	10	15	30
8	23	16	26	8	2	16	25	8	25	16	35
		17	25			17	25			17	40
Average			25	Average			25	Average			25
Maximum			27	Maximum			58	Maximum			40
Minimum			23	Minimum			2	Minimum			10
Range			4	Range			56	Range			30
Standard Deviation			1	Standard Deviation			9	Standard Deviation			10

Now our additional monitor of variability—standard deviation—should be used. Remember, this value must be used in conjunction with average.

For the three months in the table, we would draw the following conclusions. January has an average time to restore of 25 minutes and standard deviation of 1 minute, indicating that the restore times in this month are very tightly clustered. February's average restore time of 25 minutes and standard deviation of 9 minutes indicates that the restore times in this month are widely spread. March's average restore time of 25 minutes and standard deviation of 10 minutes indicates that the times in this month are also very widely spread.

For this example, when we use monitors of central tendency and variability, January is clearly different from February and March. By viewing the actual rates for February and March, we see that additional techniques may be required for analyzing these months' restore times. Using what we've learned about variability, let's revisit our call center's call volume problem.

Call Volume				
	2000	2001	2002	2003
January	2749	4081	4982	3936
February	5405	5004	4299	5024
March	3936	2708	3793	3239
April	2232	2423	1870	
May	1079	1493	1514	
June	1330	2197	1713	
July	2616	2918	1890	
August	2820	2041	1897	
September	2321	2041	1923	
October	1583	1494	1316	
November	1877	1859	1843	
December	3439	3936	2919	
Average	2616	2683	2497	4066
Range	4326	3511	3666	1785
Standard Deviation	1211	1112	1211	900

The average, range, and standard deviation work together to allow us to plan our future center needs even better. The standard deviation for the three years of 2000, 2001, and 2002 are very similar: 1,211; 1,112; and 1,211 respectively. This will allow us to conclude that our monitor of variability is a good measure. The magnitude of the standard deviation is still very high in relation to the averages, thus forcing us to plan for large swings in call volume each month.

21st Century Call Centers and Sigma

In the modern call center we must have metrics that include average to monitor central tendency and sigma to monitor variability. Understanding what sigma *is* is great, but the bigger question is, *why do I need a sigma?*

Chapter Two:
Why Sigma?

Sigma and Science

Examples of sigma use abound in the product manufacturing world. Screws and nuts really work together because product and process designers worked hard to make sure that the part variation, sigma, was held to a minimum. The concept of sigma's use in the service sector is harder to visualize. If we don't understand why we should use sigma, our use of the tool is slim. Not only do we have to use and understand sigma, additionally we must understand the science associated with its use.

To understand the concept of sigma and its scientific use, let's visit an everyday situation: the grocery store. This allows us to explain the concept of queuing theory in basic terms. For our example we have a grocery store with a checkout station. On this station we can process a full buggy load of groceries in eight minutes. One person mans the station and is paid $10,000 per year.

Now we have customers coming to the station for checkout. To make it easier to follow I have given each customer a number that will stay with them through the example scenario. This number matches when they arrived at the checkout station.

Customer 1 arrives at the checkout first, and there is no wait. Customer 2 arrives at the checkout and has to wait the eight minutes for the first person to be completed. Then the third and fourth customers both arrive with full buggies.

Customer 5 arrives and only has one item. It can be processed much faster and will only take .5 minutes or 30 seconds. Customers 6 and 7 also have one item.

In our example, we process each customer in a first-in, first-out methodology. We do not attempt to apply any of the logic associated with queuing science.

Clerk One			
Customer	**Items**	**Checkout Time**	**Wait Time**
1	Full buggy	8 min	--
2	Full buggy	8 min	8 min
3	Full buggy	8 min	16 min
4	Full buggy	8 min	24 min
5	One item	.5 min	32 min
6	One item	.5 min	32.5 min
7	One item	.5 min	33 min

In the table we see the queue—or line—at the checkout with the corresponding processing time and wait time respectively. The average processing time is 4.8 minutes. The processing time sigma is 4.0 minutes.

We can easily see that the wait times are getting out of hand and totally unacceptable to our customers. When one clerk is used our average wait is 24.25 minutes with a sigma of 10.36 minutes. This wait time is excessive and our store manager must do something to improve the situation.

But in our example no thought is given to the impact of sigma, and we crudely overpower the wait time by adding more clerks.

Our crude solution to resolving the long wait times at the register is to add more clerks. The clerks will process the customers through the checkout line in a first-in, first-out manner. Our store manager adds one additional clerk, and the resulting queues are shown in the table below.

Clerk One			
Customer	**Items**	**Checkout Time**	**Wait Time**
1	Full buggy	8 min	
3	Full buggy	8 min	8 min
5	One item	.5 min	16 min
7	One item	.5 min	16.5 min

Clerk Two			
Customer	**Items**	**Checkout Time**	**Wait Time**
2	Full buggy	8 min	
4	Full buggy	8 min	8 min
6	One item	.5 min	16 min

With two clerks processing at checkout, our average wait is 12.9 minutes. This solution has reduced the average wait time, but it has increased our cost since we now have two clerks making $10,000 each. Our total cost is $20,000.

The wait time is still somewhat high, so our store manager decides to open a third line. The table below shows the impact on the wait time for each customer.

Clerk One			
Customer	**Items**	**Checkout Time**	**Wait Time**
1	Full buggy	8 min	
4	Full buggy	8 min	8 min
7	One item	.5 min	16 min

Clerk Two			
Customer	**Items**	**Checkout Time**	**Wait Time**
2	Full buggy	8 min	
5	One item	.5 min	8 min

Clerk Three			
Customer	**Items**	**Checkout Time**	**Wait Time**
3	Full buggy	8 min	
6	One item	.5 min	8 min

With three clerks, the average wait drops to 10.0 minutes. This approach carries a $30,000 price tag.

Express Lane Structure

If we understand queuing science, we know that wait time is impacted by things other than just adding people. Rethinking the whole grocery store checkout methodology can yield some interesting results. In this example, we see that wait time is also a function of average processing time and the processing time variability. Variability is the size difference of our checkout time. The lower the difference, the lower the wait time. Let's look again at our grocery store checkout example, but this time split our customers into two groups. One group has full buggies and members of the other group have one item each. The processing time variability for each group is zero. The processing time of the full buggy line is eight minutes. The processing time of the one item line is .5 minutes.

The result of this shift in method is shown in the table below.

Full Buggy Clerk			
Customer	**Items**	**Checkout Time**	**Wait Time**
1	Full buggy	8 min	
2	Full buggy	8 min	8 min
3	Full buggy	8 min	16 min
4	Full buggy	8 min	24 min

Express Clerk			
Customer	Items	Checkout Time	Wait Time
5	One item	.5 min	
6	One item	.5 min	.5 min
7	One item	.5 min	1.0 min

With one full buggy clerk and an express lane clerk, the average wait drops to 9.9 minutes with a cost of $20,000.

Efficient Versus Effective

Now let's compare the two grocery store approaches. The crude but *efficient* grocery store has the three clerks fully loaded. The average wait is 10 minutes and the cost is $30,000. The *effective* grocery store has a new method and structure. The effective grocery store takes a different approach of balancing both the store's needs and the customer's needs by using queuing science. The queuing science approach looks at the other drivers of wait time: average processing, processing time sigma, and utilization. One clerk is processing full buggies and the second clerk is processing one-item customers using an express lane. With this approach the average wait is 9.9 minutes and the cost is $20,000.

The table below compares our crude approach to the express lane approach where queuing science has been applied and sigma has been minimized.

	Crude Approach	Express Lane Approach
Number of clerks	3 clerks	2 clerks
Cost	$30,000	$20,000
Wait time Average	10 minutes	9.9 minutes

In every aspect of the above example the express lane approach is better. Our express lane may not be *efficient* at the micro level (on occasion our express clerk might have to wait for a customer with the requisite low number of groceries), but the total store is more *effective* using the express lane approach.

Express Lanes Work Because of Sigma

The reason grocery store express lanes work is the underlying queuing science and the management of sigma. Note in the table below the difference in sigma from the crude design approach to the express lane approach. Grocery stores spent decades before they understood how important sigma was.

	Crude Approach	Express Lane Approach	
		Full Service	Express Lane
Processing Time Average	4.8 minutes	8.0 minutes	.5 minutes
Processing Time Sigma	4.0 minutes	0.0 minutes	0.0 minutes

One of the ironies of call center design and management is that one of the key drivers is sigma, and virtually no one is even looking at sigma.

Balance

To achieve production, quality, and satisfy our customers we must meet the three quality objectives:

- Wait time
- Cost
- Performance

With these three criteria, we have a clear call center goal. We must now marshal our efforts to achieve the target.

Many times I hear the question, *Do you want quantity or quality?* Production or "quantity," is often mistakenly defined as keeping all agents busy, getting callers off the lines, or the number of calls handled. The only correct time to count production is when we answer the customer question perfectly, he pays us, and he is happy. The only answer to the question above, *Do you want quality or quantity?* is that we want both quantity and quality.

Clearly, our definition of quality is extremely broad and encompassing. According to our definition, quality is comprised of three components:

performance, cost, and time. Our research, analysis, and decisions must support the goal of delighting our customers (performance), while reducing our cost (cost), and providing our product to our customers the moment they want it (time). We must view this goal as a never-ending journey to continue improving all three components because no one component is more important than the others. All three must be viewed with equal importance and balance.

Often I hear people say that you can have one or two of the three criteria of wait time, cost, and performance. To achieve all three, creative application of science is required.

Sigma and Science in a Call Center

These numbers are call center phone pickup time measurements. The central tendency (average) is .0499. It is the balance point of the values and is shown in the chart below.

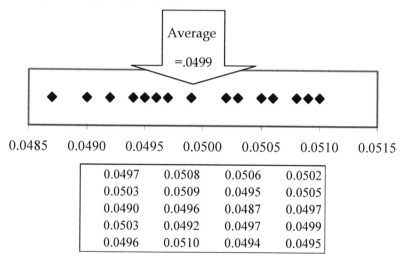

0.0497	0.0508	0.0506	0.0502
0.0503	0.0509	0.0495	0.0505
0.0490	0.0496	0.0487	0.0497
0.0503	0.0492	0.0497	0.0499
0.0496	0.0510	0.0494	0.0495

Variability is monitored by range and standard deviation. The chart below shows the range for the phone pickup time measurements.

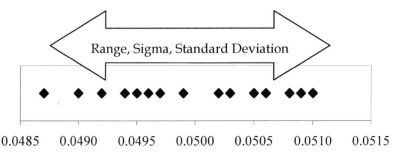

| 0.0485 | 0.0490 | 0.0495 | 0.0500 | 0.0505 | 0.0510 | 0.0515 |

Wait time is a function of processing time average, processing time variability, and agent utilization. Average monitors the central tendency, and standard deviation monitors the variability. This chart shows an average processing time of three minutes and associated sigma monitored by standard deviations. One standard deviation is small and the other is larger.

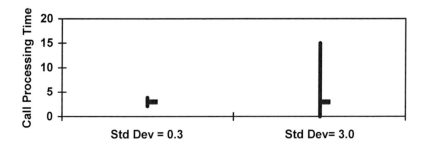

Note that 99.8% of calls with the low variation of 0.3 minutes will fall between two and four minutes processing time. The range is derived from a probability calculation. It is important to understand the spread of the calls and their impact on wait time.

The range of 99.8% of the calls with the larger variation of 3.0 minutes will fall between zero and 15 minutes processing time. This spread will have a large wait time if all the other drivers are kept stable.

The next chart shows a third standard deviation of 30 minutes, which is a large amount of variability for an average processing time of three minutes.

Average Call Processing Time of 3 minutes

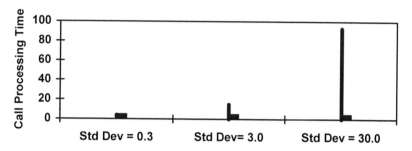

This new larger spread will have between zero and 90 minutes processing time for 99.8% of calls with the larger variation of 30.0 minutes standard deviation. This spread will have a larger wait time if all the other drivers are kept stable.

Wait time is a function of processing time, utilization, and processing time sigma or variability. The equation that computes wait time from these three is called Pollaczek-Kyntchin equation. For more details on queuing science and its application in the world of call centers and help desks read *Designing Effective Call Centers*.

Using the wait time equation, we can compute wait time. The chart below shows two scenarios, each with an average processing time of 3.0 minutes. One situation has a low sigma of .3 minutes and the other has a high sigma of 30.0 minutes. The high variability situation's wait time increases at a much higher rate than the low variability case.

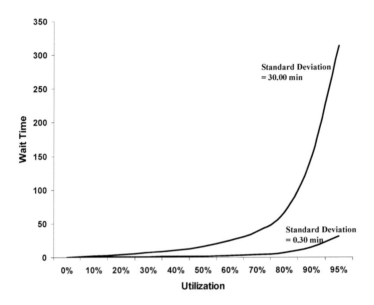

Queuing Science

Queuing science allows us to *have it all* through an understanding of processing time average and sigma. The closer the processing times are to each other, the lower the wait time. Standard deviation is a measure of sigma. The closer the sigma variability (monitored by standard deviation) is to zero, the less difference in our checkout times.

Now we will apply what we learned in the grocery store example to call centers. In the 1910s when the first call centers were built all operators did the exact same routing task, thus all calls were about the same duration. Call variation stayed a non-issue for decades. With the advent of modern centers with multiple tasks, call processing time variation became a major issue.

Today we have the five call center types—routing, notification, call management, processing, and content dissemination. Science and metrics allow us to determine what could form a call center express lane. These call center express lanes keep wait times down, reduce cost, and provide better performance in our responses to customers or users.

The grocery store checkout example showed the impact of the drivers of wait time. Wait time is a function of the utilization of the clerk, the processing time average, and the processing time variability. The Pollaczek-Kyntchin equation takes all three issues into account and calculates wait time. In a modern call center, caller waits are a function of agent utilization, call processing time average, and call processing time variability.

The graph below shows us the wait time results. The horizontal axis of the graph shows utilizations from 0% to 100%. The vertical axis shows the calculated wait time from 0 minutes to 350 minutes. The line graph shown is for a call that has an average processing time of three minutes. The call processing time variation is from two minutes to four minutes. The spread is relatively small.

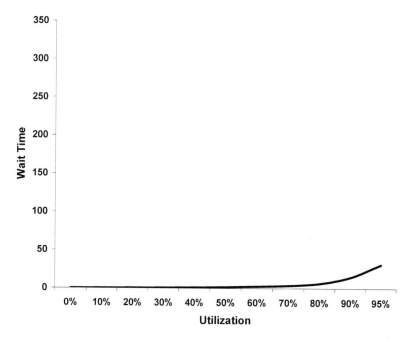

The curve stays very close to zero and only begins to rise as we approach 90+% utilization. With most calls being close to the average, our wait times are low and manageable.

Next we will use the same graph but add one more curve. The second curve is the dashed line. It represents the change in variability from call to call. This call-to-call variation produces a larger spread around the average processing time of three minutes. The call variation for one call may go as high as 15 minutes and then drop to zero minutes. The processing time for an individual call is between zero and 15 minutes.

As the spread from call to call increases, the wait times begin to grow past 70% utilization. Comparing the first curve with minimal call processing time variation to the second situation with higher variation, we see that we must have lower utilizations to keep the comparable wait times of the low variation.

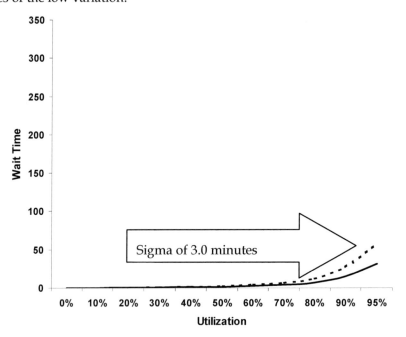

A third curve is added to our graph. This curve has a very wide spread between calls. The curve represents an extremely high variability ranging from 90 minutes down to zero minutes. The call processing time for an individual call will be somewhere between the zero minute and 90 minute spread.

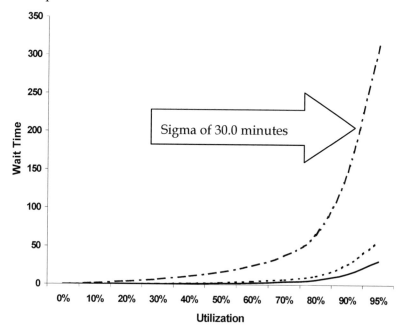

As the spread from call to call increases, the wait times begin to grow past 30% utilization, and the curve shows wait times increasing rapidly. Comparing the first curve with minimal call processing time variation to the second situation with moderate variation, we see that we must have lower utilizations to keep the comparable wait times of the low variation. When we include high variation, the agent utilization must be low.

Call Processing: 3 Minutes			
Call Variation	Low	Moderate	High
Call Sigma	.3 minutes	3.0 Minutes	30 minutes
Agent Utilization	80%	60%	20%
Caller Wait Time	4 minutes	4 minutes	4 minutes

The table above shows a comparison of variations and their impact on wait time, agent utilization, and cost.

In the grocery store example, by understanding the wait-time drivers and building express lanes that took the processing time average, processing time sigma, and utilization into account, we were able to reduce cost, reduce wait time, and provide better service. The same principles can be applied in the call center.

One closing concept. Variation is the spread of the measurements of a metric. Sigma is the value of this variation if we had all the information about the complete source or population. Standard deviation is our estimate of the value of the sigma. Technically there is a difference between the terms variation, sigma, and standard deviation, but each, in its special way, is tracking the metric measurement spread.

Chapter Three:
Sigma Designs in a Call Center

Effective six sigma call centers and help desks must be scientifically engineered. Let's go back to our grocery store example. A very effective manager can still have a store that is not effective. If our store is set up according to the crude model, with all clerks doing every job and not minimizing the processing time variability, the store manager can only add or remove clerks. The store manager can only be as effective as the store design.

The irony in this example is that it took 70 years for grocery store chains to appreciate the need to monitor and manage processing time variability. Can we really expect the store manager to develop effective aisle flows, product placement, pricing, discounts, AND to design or redesign the store? An effective store design must be strategically engineered.

The store manager should expect that the store has already been well designed and engineered. Our call center managers should expect the same. The call center design must be periodically reevaluated to assure that our engineering design is still adequate for the policy vision.

My **four traits of effective operations** are the ability to respond to rapid change, a factored organizational structure (express lanes) supported by defined processes, a competent workforce that brilliantly executes the plan, and optimum decision-making based on proper information. Strategic engineering is required for the first two traits-- responding to rapid change and express lanes with defined processes. The last two traits (brilliant execution and optimal decision-making) help the tactical decision-makers to manage the scientifically engineered call center. With a well-engineered store checkout or call center we can expect our operation to be managed effectively.

Engineering provides the strategic facility that matches the policy vision. Operations must provide a competent workforce to brilliantly execute the plan. To run an effective operation the managers must trust the strategic engineers to have done their job well. Any decision-making must be based on proper information, better known as metrics. Metrics must always monitor both central tendency and sigma.

Call centers reside in a rapid, changing, dynamic world. The environment requires timely, focused, and appropriate information. The change management philosophy allows us to use the tactician to detect change so that once we have a strategic baseline we only have to reassess the center when a change occurs. These changes must be assessed immediately, so that each change can be managed.

We cannot manage a metric like abandonment—we can only react to it. We must understand the drivers and then manage those drivers. These metric drivers must have a decision support structure for proactive decisions.

Metrics and Science

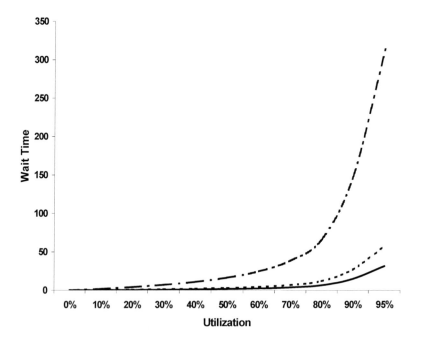

Grocery store designers and managers built new and better techniques based on metrics and science. Call center strategic decision-makers must also use metrics, a metric blueprint, and science to build and manage state of the art call centers. As an example, our proactive strategic decision-maker understands that we must manage processing time central tendency, processing time variability, and agent utilization to manage wait time and abandonment.

Strategists and Tacticians

Peak efficiency is dependent on strategists providing a correct and capable facility, which includes both physical and intellectual assets. The tactical work force must count on the strategic players to uphold their end of the bargain.

Providing the call center facility is clearly strategic and the job of the strategic decision-maker. These strategic decisions are

- Providing the tools, methods, structure, and technology to meet the policy vision of the executive.

- Assessing the impact on the customer or user when a change in the process and product metrics has occurred.

- Dynamically retooling the center to meet business changes.

Since strategy and tactics are very different, a different metric view for each seems logical. The tactical view supports the need to detect a change. The strategic metric view supports the assessment of how well the center is performing, as a function of the customer's needs.

Our strategic reports will look at each of the following:
- Grouping
- Metric Description
  - Central Tendency
  - Variability
  - Distribution
- Predictions

Failure to monitor all three characteristics as a team will lead to catastrophic mistakes. Grouping, metric description, and predictions form an essential team that allows us to vividly understand, monitor, and make informed decisions about our call centers.

Segmentation for Reduced Sigma

There are three segmentation types: 1) Physical, 2) Associational, and 3) Time-series. **Physical** groups are those groups that are physically of like kind. **Associational** groups are physically the same but form groups because the analytical numbers are different. **Time-series** groups are from groups over time.

Homogeneous groups may seem obvious to one person and not to another. Thus clear guidelines are required. Control is another way of saying homogeneous or consistent. We must never allow a mixture of non-homogeneous groups. We cannot mix size 12 and size 9 shoes together in a homogeneous group. Neither can we mix blue shirts with white shirts. An average of a size 10½ shoe or a pale blue shirt would be misleading. Instead, simple common sense is required to properly prepare homogeneous groups. It appears to be obvious to keep groups separate, but this is not always the case. Grouping requirements may be difficult to conceptualize and even harder to assure.

Call centers require segmenting the business, operation, products, process, time, skill, users, content, exposure, etc.

Call Center Design with No Thought to Sigma

The crude approach to the operation of a call center or help desk forces all calls to one non-homogeneous group. For an example, we will use the National Candy Company IT help desk. The National Candy Company help desk includes desktop support, product support, billing applications, point of sales support, and network support. All requests go to one pool of general IT representatives who are supposed to respond to every type of question and request.

The following table shows the processing time of calls into the IT help desk. The help desk's calls are processed in a first in first out manner. The following table shows the processing time of the call cases.

National Candy Company IT Help Desk Processing Time by Case									
Case		Case		Case		Case		Case	
1	17.55	15	207.00	29	26.40	43	132.00	57	20.50
2	114.00	16	20.20	30	101.00	44	36.05	58	18.75
3	35.70	17	39.00	31	26.70	45	26.65	59	27.00
4	18.00	18	20.45	32	26.70	46	182.00	60	27.45
5	18.35	19	36.20	33	26.78	47	37.25	61	20.19
6	125.00	20	20.65	34	39.40	48	37.35	62	20.70
7	18.50	21	157.00	35	27.11	49	38.30	63	18.00
8	156.00	22	20.85	36	176.00	50	38.40	64	21.25
9	19.15	23	182.00	37	27.20	51	137.00	65	21.10
10	19.25	24	21.10	38	27.25	52	20.25	66	27.20
11	19.65	25	21.20	39	27.35	53	39.55	67	18.45
12	19.65	26	147.00	40	199.00	54	40.54	68	37.25
13	19.68	27	21.25	41	27.90	55	40.80	69	17.60
14	19.70	28	21.30	42	27.95	56	43.60	70	98.00

If all calls are lumped together with no grouping, the average and standard deviation of call volume would be 51.22 and 52.94 respectively. The following chart shows the distribution of the National Candy Company help desk call processing time. Each bar shows the number of calls for each processing time group.

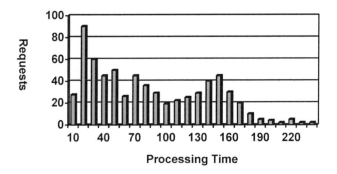

Using the National Candy IT help desk call processing time of an average of 51.22 and sigma of 52.94, derived from the crude center model, the following chart shows the processing time. Note the steep and rapid slope of the wait-time curve.

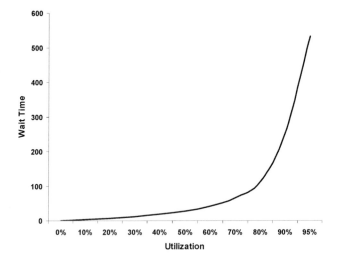

The scale of the y-axis ranges from 0 to 600 minutes. As the utilization increases the wait time rapidly grows. The slope of the wait time curve dramatically increases. The curve's slope continues to grow more sharply as the utilization increases.

This crude model leaves us with few choices other than keeping a low utilization to maintain any reasonable customer or user wait time.

Designing with Sigma in Mind

First let's rethink our crude model that lumps all the calls together and look for a way to reduce sigma. If we organize the processing time into functional groups we see the table below. The following table shows the processing time of each call type flowing into the IT help desk. The help desk's call support types are desktop, product support, billing, sales, and networking.

Desktop	Product Support	Billing	Sales	Network
17.55	20.19	26.40	35.70	101.00
17.60	20.20	26.65	36.05	125.00
18.00	20.25	26.70	36.20	156.00
18.00	20.45	26.70	37.25	182.00
18.35	20.50	26.78	37.25	182.00
18.45	20.65	27.00	37.35	137.00
18.50	20.70	27.11	38.30	199.00
18.75	20.85	27.20	38.40	207.00
19.15	21.10	27.20	39.00	132.00
19.25	21.10	27.25	39.40	147.00
19.65	21.20	27.35	39.55	176.00
19.65	21.25	27.45	40.54	157.00
19.68	21.25	27.90	40.80	114.00
19.70	21.30	27.95	43.60	98.00

When the calls were lumped together with no grouping, the average and standard deviation of call volume would be 51.22 and 52.94 respectively. The five call types have their grouped results calculated below.

	All Type	Desk-top	Product Sup-port	Billing	Sales	Net-work
Average	51.22	18.73	20.79	27.12	38.53	150.93
Standard Deviation	52.94	.78	.42	.46	2.17	35.05
N	70	14	14	14	14	14

First note that four of the five case types processing time averages are significantly lower than the all-type average. Note that each group's sigma is radically lower than the overall sigma of 52.94.

Each product type's call processing time is plotted on the graph below. For some groups, the individual call processing time is so similar that the plot points almost take the form of one large point while the networking area is very diverse and each network processing time varies.

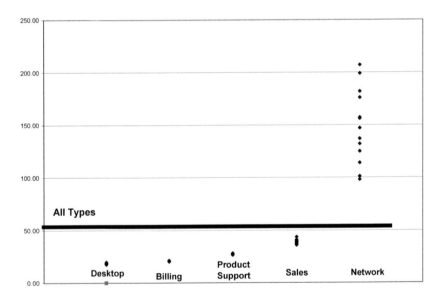

Grouping the calls together while ignoring the analytical differences makes the average worthless. This can be seen visually on the scatter plot above. The average for all types is shown as a straight line horizontally across the graph. The all-type average is not close to any value and is useless. Also, the all-type standard deviation (52.94) is radically larger than any of the individual groups' standard deviation (desktop .78, product support .42, billing .46, sales 2.17, and network 35.05). Using the all-type standard deviation would create the erroneous impression of much higher variability than is truly the case. Separate studies should be done for each group.

Having found a way to reduce the variability is great, but how do we put that information to work to improve our center? Let's take a look at the desktop support requests and see what the processing time average of 18.73 and the sigma of .78 does to our queues and wait time. Below is the desktop support distribution. Note that the large arrow is the location of the lumped average and how the desktop distribution has nothing in relation to the desktop average.

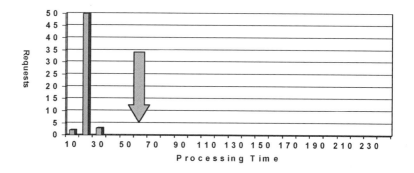

Using the P-K equation with the desktop function's processing time average of 18.73 minutes, and a sigma of .78 minutes, we can compute wait times for each agent's utilization from 0% to 100%. The wait time curve is shown below.

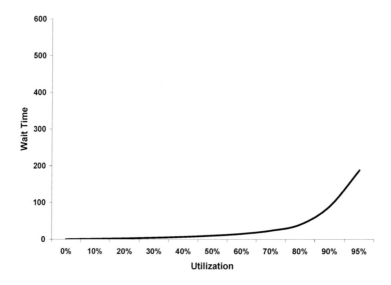

Note how the wait-time curve for the desktop support express lane is much flatter than the crude model all-type help desk curve.

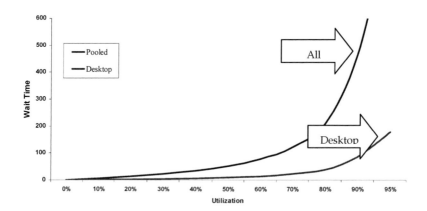

Now, comparing the lumped wait-time curve and the desktop support curve, we see a huge difference.

The crude model all type compared to the desktop express lane shows that the same wait time requires a huge utilization difference.

Now let's analyze another segment of the call center. The product support requests shown below have a processing time average of 20.79

minutes and a sigma of .42 minutes. Note that the large arrow is the location of the lumped average and how the product support distribution has nothing in relation to the overall average.

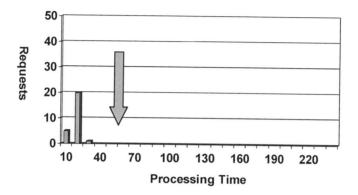

Below is the distribution for each one of the functions.

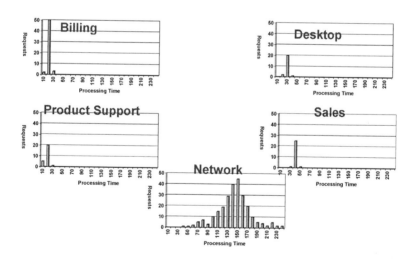

When we use the P-K equation for each of the help desk segments, the following five wait time curves can be developed.

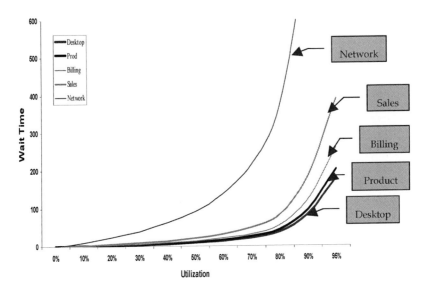

The desktop, product support, billing, and sales wait-time curves are significantly lower than the original all type pooled curve. The network group's wait time curve is higher than the all type curve. You can see this results in the graph below.

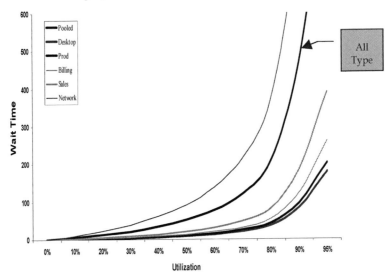

With a well thought out call center sigma design and a management plan we can have significantly higher utilization. The end result will allow lower cost, lower wait times, and better performance.

Sigma designs benefits include

- Lower wait time
- Better satisfaction
- Targeted SLAs
- Higher utilization
- Lower cost
- Better service
- Happier staff
- Better coefficient of value

Why Six?

Our definition of **Six Sigma** is *having or making a product or service that is virtually flawless each and every time.* Now we need a more in depth explanation. Everyone has been graded on a bell-shaped curve at some point during their schooling. The bell curve's other names are the normal distribution or the Gaussian distribution. The normal distribution is used to convert the actual grades or test scores to a letter grade.

The normal distribution is where the idea of six sigma came from. Let's dig into and understand the normal distribution. Normal distribution is described with the average as the central point of the measurements, and the standard deviation is the variability of the measurements. The normal distribution is symmetric around its average. Fifty percent of the data points are above the average and fifty percent of the measurements are below the average. The frequency of occurrence (or the number of occurrences) drops rapidly as we move farther and farther away from the center. This characteristic is true both above and below the average. The frequency of occurrences above and below the average is symmetric.

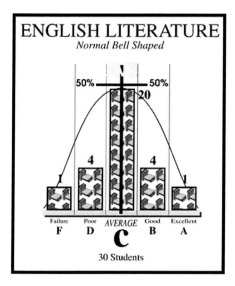

ENGLISH LITERATURE
Normal Bell Shaped

This chart is used to depict a picture of how a process with its measurements will look. The chart shows the spread of grades from an English literature class of thirty students. When the score measurements are converted to grades and look like the diagram, the process is well represented by a normal distribution. The perfect normal does not have the steps of a histogram but is a smooth curve.

Why is the Normal Distribution Important?

Having data that is well represented by a normal distribution allows us to predict using the probabilities of the normal. Because a good understanding of these probabilities is essential, let's now look at them in more detail.

The previous chart shows how a typical class in English literature could have been graded using a bell-shaped curve. Out of a class of 30 students, 20 would receive a "C", four would receive a "B", another four would receive a "D", one would receive an "A", and one would receive an "F".

The normal distribution helps us make projections for assessing the center, check for proper groups, and assess whether the center is running correctly and consistently. These issues allow us to reduce wait time, provide better service, and reduce cost. To keep the facility running at its optimum, these issues have continued importance. For this chapter the making of projections is our focus. A few examples of call center and help desk projections are:

- Staffing
- Call volume
- Utilization
- Backlog of open calls

To staff our facility based on call processing time could enhance our center. In years past we staffed to the average processing time and this worked well for us as long as the variability was small. In today's modern center variability is a very real issue. Using the past practice of average processing time as our staffing base line, our center is understaffed half the time. The magnitude of this understaffing is directly related to the magnitude of the variability. Being able to make sound predictions will allow the strategists to accomplish their role

51

much more effectively. In a scientifically engineered center, metrics can fill this prediction need.

The metric being represented by a normal distribution allows us to predict using the probabilities of the normal. Resolving these issues allows us to reduce wait time, provide better service, and reduce cost. Now we need to learn the normal probabilities so that we can use them for predictions.

Predicting Operational Results

All measurements that track like a normal distribution have a very definite set of probabilities. Since the normal distribution is symmetric, the probabilities above and below the average are exactly the same.

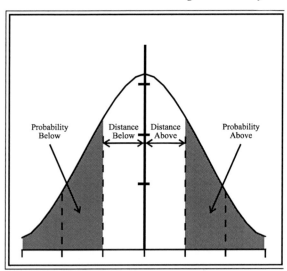

This chart shows the symmetry when the distance above and below the average is equal. When the distances are equal, the area under the normal curve is the same above and below the average. Since the bell is symmetrical, we can focus our attention on the "distance above" side, because the same calculations and probability will apply for the "distance below" side.

As the distance away from the mean, or center, of a normal distribution gets bigger, the probability gets smaller.

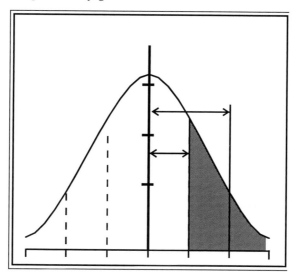

Due to the normal distribution's symmetry, only one formula is required and the sign is always positive. To have a general equation for all measurements we must convert this distance to a ratio. The ratio will be the distance as a function of variability. This ratio will remove units of measure such as the pickup time and will give us a conversion factor that all measurements can use. For details see your metrics analyst or read *Preparing Call Center Metrics.*

Z is the ratio of the distance away from the average as a function of variability measured by standard deviation. This Z value, which is a ratio, allows the use of one probability table for any measurement.

Now this table is used to locate the probability for the particular Z value that has been computed. This table shows us the relationship of distances away from the average. The ratio of the distances away from the average, or Z, allows us to determine the probability from the point out.

The distance away from the average as a function of the metric standard deviation or Z	Probability outside the point	Percent of the call center outside a point
1	16%	16 out of 100
2	2.3%	2.3 out of 100
3	.1%	1 out of 1,000
4	.003%	3 out of 100,000
5	.00003%	3 out of 10 million
6	.0000001%	1 out of 1 billion

In the table above, a Z value of six gives a probability of .000000001 or one out of a billion occurrences. A Z value of four gives a probability of .00003, or three out of 100,000 occurrences. A Z value of three yields a probability of .00135 or 1.35 out of 1,000 occurrences. A Z value of two yields a probability of 2.28 out of 100. A Z value of one gives a probability of .1587 or 15.87 out of 100 occurrences, while a Z value of zero yields a 50 times out of 100 occurrence rate.

Expanding the prediction area we can build a table that will show spots where our center metrics will fall. Now we can use these predictions in our center and support the strategic role of assessing the center capability.

Six Sigma

Our simple definition of six sigma stated having and making a flawless product or service. For me, flawless is another way of saying perfection and one out of a billion is pretty much that perfection. Now we can quantity our definition of six sigma as a level of one out of a billion failures.

Here are some examples of why I want the level to be high. When I am on an airplane, I really want the odds of a failure to be very low. When we are looking at a complex system like an airplane, computer network, or a 21st century call center, for the system to work, all the components must work flawlessly. As the number of components in a complex system increases, this causes the system's reliability to decrease. From a study of probability where all the components must work together in a system, the reliability probabilities of each component must be multiplied together to arrive at the system reliability probability. The idea of six sigma is to provide a buffer so that when things happen (and they will) we still have our flawless operation.

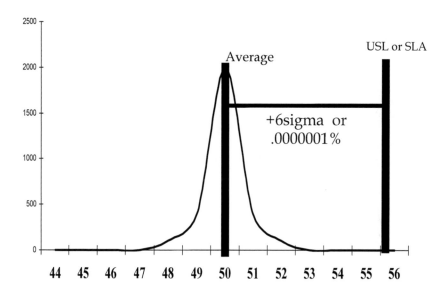

Now, when the unexpected happens and the average shifts, we have a buffer that still keeps us in good shape.

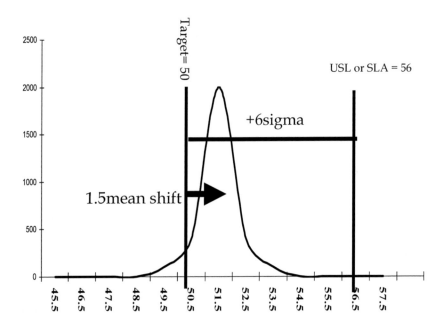

In the graph above the call center process or product metric has shifted with a magnitude of 1.5 sigma. This shift leaves us with a remaining 4.5 sigma, or Z, from the specification limit or service level agreement. Expanding the prediction area we can build a table that will show spots where our call center metrics will fall.

% of Calls Exceeding SLA	# of Calls Exceeding SLA	Z
50%	1 out of 2	0
30%	3 out of 10	.53
16%	16 out of 100	1
2.3%	2.3 out of 100	2
.1%	1 out of 1,000	3
.003%	3 out of 100,000	4
.0003%	**3 out of 1 million**	**4.5**
.00003%	3 out of 10 million	5
.0000001%	1 out of 1 billion	6

Now we can use these predictions in our call center and support the strategic role of assessing the center capability and assure that we never have a problem. Even when we do have a large shift of the mean, like 1.5 sigma, we are still in good shape with a three out of a million probability of exceeding the specification limit or service level agreement.

Using the Normal Table for Risk Management

We make decisions on information we've prepared as well as we can, but there's always a chance that our information is flawed. For our purposes here, risk management is the risk that our decision-making information is flawed. The following show the formula adjustments required.

Not only can the normal table be used to compute probability, this process can be reversed to compute a probability of risk where we arrive at the spots where this amount of risk would occur.

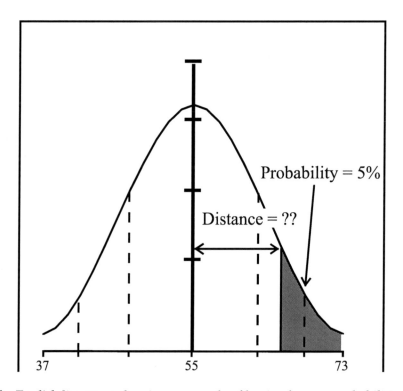

The English literature class is an example of having known probabilities and arriving at the number of occurrences or the particular spot.

It is the role of the strategist to decide how much risk of excessive wait time we're willing to take. Our strategic decision-maker decides that we will take a 5% risk of a call taking longer than the computed (X_i) time to process. The 5% is converted to .05. For example, let's compute the pickup time range where 90% of the calls' pickup time falls inside this calculated range. Stated another way, the risk is 5% being above the upper range point and the risk is 5% being below the lower calculated point.

Expanding the prediction area we can build a table that will show spots where our call center metrics will fall.

% of Calls Exceeding SLA	# of Calls Exceeding SLA	Z
50%	1 out of 2	0
30%	3 out of 10	.53
16%	16 out of 100	1
10%	10 out of 100	1.28
5%	5 out of 100	1.645
2.3%	2.3 out of 100	2
.1%	1 out of 1,000	3
.003%	3 out of 100,000	4
.00003%	3 out of 10 million	5
.0000001%	1 out of 1 billion	6

Now you can have your designer or analyst use these predictions in our call center and support the strategic role of assessing the center capability. Your designer or analyst can also calculate and predict the call volume, center staffing, talk time, etc.

Now we have the tools to design, run, and maintain an optimal center with a clear understanding of why we use a sigma of six in our designs.

Chapter Five:

Starting a Six Sigma Design

Vision

The **Second Principle of Process Management** states that *Division of Labor is the framework for all aspects of decision making. It must be clearly understood to separate the policy, strategic, and tactical decisions. Operations makes the tactical decisions of running the facility. Management makes the strategic decisions of assessing the facility's suitability for the job. **Executives make the policy decisions of providing the vision for the business.***

Peak efficiency requires a clear vision with the strategist providing a correct and capable facility. Our tactical workforce must count on the strategic players to deliver their end of the bargain.

Providing the business and call center vision is the job of the policy decision-maker. These policy decisions are

- Providing the policy vision of the business.
- Determining how we will treat our customers.

A student, after attending one of my classes, wrote and asked a really profound question. "I understand the concepts, the principles, and techniques, but how do I get started?" As he realized, getting started is key.

First we must establish a clear vision. Let's imagine that we are starting a design for changing automobile tires. I regularly ask people how long it would take them to change one tire on their car. I hear times ranging from 15 minutes to three hours. Using these past practices, if I take the shortest time of 15 minutes and extend that for all four tires, I would have to plan for at least an hour to change the tires. Now imagine that we are a racing team and this hour would be our pit stop time plus another ten minutes to add gas. How competitive would our team be?

Our vision must reflect where we are going and not be restricted to where we are or where we have been. Vision is not limited by capability or cost. It should be a statement of where we would like to be. Our strategist will be charged with developing the plan. If our racing team had started with a limited vision, we would never achieve a 15 second pit stop, four tires changed, and a full tank of gas. NASCAR teams must beat that time just to be in the race.

Our first step is to clear our heads of any preconceived ideas and start with a clean sheet of paper. We don't want to get caught up in what our facility can do or how it is being done. Our vision must be a statement of where we would like to be and what perfection would be. Yogi Berra is quoted as saying, "If you don't know where you are going, you might wind up someplace else." We must know where we want to go before anything else can be developed.

Paradigm

The proper objective background against which to consider a problem is the sum of all human knowledge. It is especially true in technical fields that this "frontier of knowledge" moves rapidly. An engineer educated a few years ago may be busily redesigning and perfecting vacuum tube circuits, unaware of the properties and potential of solid state devices. This used to be called a provincial view, implying geographic isolation. The idea has been updated to describe the intellectual isolation of someone who falls behind in a particular field of specialized knowledge. Such a movement and changing terrain of knowledge is called a paradigm shift. A paradigm is our current state of knowledge or understanding.

While traveling in Germany, I had an opportunity to rent a car and drive on the German highway system. Having learned how to drive in the United States, I brought what I considered excellent skill and knowledge of driving with me. My first venture onto the German highway system was on the Autobahn leaving Munich. United States driver's training teaches that speed kills and that 65 miles per hour is safe. I began my journey from Munich, but I could not determine my miles per hour because all measurements were in kilometers per hour.

A new set of skills became very important. First, I learned that slow drivers should always stay to the right. Fast drivers always stay to the left. If you are a slow driver and need to pass, you check for vehicles rapidly approaching from the rear, pass quickly, and immediately return to the right lane. You do not weave in and out of traffic. This is the standard German approach to driving. I felt much safer on the Autobahn than driving on US interstates even though I had no idea of how fast I was driving. I stayed pretty much with the flow of traffic, letting conditions and traffic flow dictate my speed. When I arrived at my destination, I was astounded to find that I had been driving at 100 miles per hour consistently for a long period of time. My paradigm had changed from speed kills to speed is actually safer. We must continually reassess our perspective.

Defining the Vision

First we must define and document our business, operation, or center vision. This will become our guiding light. Defining the vision requires that we answer the following questions: Who are our users and customers? What are their segments or how should they be organized and subdivided? How many users and customers do we have? How do our customers want to contact us? How does our organization want to treat them?

Next we must find out what services we are going to provide. Are we going to do routing, notification, call management, processing or content dissemination?

If we are providing call management the center will act as the agent of the users and customers so we must track and monitor each request from front to back.

When we have established what we will provide we must then state when we will provide the service to them and what level of service we will provide.

This becomes the center vision statement that includes the following key components:

- **Performance**
  - What are the functions
  - Who do we support and how do we treat them
- **Time**
  - When do we provide the services
- **Cost**
  - How much could we afford to spend

This written vision statement is no more than a page and is preferably a paragraph. With our background, or homework, completed, we are ready to begin product and process design for our center. Our homework is the documentation and validation of assumptions and paradigm.

Using the Vision

Now our strategist is ready to start building the facility. A clear understanding of the Principles of Process Management is mandatory to everything we will do. The First Principle of Process Management plays a crucial role in improvement.

First Principle of Process Management

A fundamental understanding of BOTH the product and process is essential to improvement. Both the product and the process must be described and understood individually and separately. *The underlying component for improving the product is the process.*

There are two broad areas in which you may collect data. These areas are product and process. In general, it helps to have data from each area.

A product is…	• Noun • Result	When we are discussing products, we are focusing on the result of our activities. The product is always a noun.	**Product**
A process is…	• Verb • Activity • Something that builds the product	Process discussions are focused on the activities that build the product. The process is always a verb.	**Process**

Because the product is the goal and objective, many people monitor only the product. This would be like the coach of a football team only looking at the scoreboard to make all his play-calling decisions. An equal knowledge of the process is required to achieve the goal. Actually, the football coach must monitor all aspects of the game including the line play, the quarterback's execution, the receiver's speed, and the back's running. The complete set of information allows the coach to make an accurate call for the next play.

Many people have difficulty making a clear distinction between product and process. The important issue is to monitor both with equal fervor because overemphasis on either one will result in mistakes. To clarify the difference between product and process, please let me use a personal illustration.

Grandma's Biscuits

Growing up in Tennessee, I developed a fond appreciation of family. My grandparents were some of the wisest people I've ever met. My grandmother in particular was the bedrock of the family. She held a full-time job as a first grade teacher and raised a wonderful family. That job alone included many diverse aspects and activities, but she was brilliant in every way in meeting the challenges that confronted her. She had all the positive traits of a southern lady (grace, charm, uplifting personality, intelligence, and so on). I never heard her say an unkind word, and she never raised her voice, but she was still able to get her objectives and agenda accomplished.

One southern trait that was essential was the ability to bake biscuits. Wow, did my grandmother's biscuits taste fantastic! They were light and fluffy--the best-tasting thing that you have ever put in your mouth! Twice a day she baked these biscuits, and twice a day they were always perfect. My grandmother cooked the finest biscuits in the world, and people came from near and far to taste them. What made my grandmother even more special was that even when she went to the cupboard and ingredients were missing, she simply changed the recipe. Voila!!...she still had perfect biscuits. In recorded time, she never made a bad batch of biscuits.

Later, my mother, who also is the salt of the earth and a perfect southern lady, began to follow in my grandmother's footsteps. She had a desire to bake delicious biscuits too, so she watched my grandmother for about two months. After closely observing, my mother felt ready to make her first batch of biscuits. We were all excited the first morning that she tried her new skills, and we could hardly wait to taste the finished product. To our shock and dismay, we found that they were burnt to a crisp! Meal after meal, my mother diligently worked and worked at making good biscuits. No matter how hard she tried, the burnt biscuits continued for weeks. Eventually the family realized something had to be done, so we began to build a set of measurements and reports about burnt biscuits. After two more months, we had a wealth of information about burnt biscuits but no information about good biscuits. Finally, the happy day arrived when my mother made a perfect batch of biscuits. We knew that she had made a technical breakthrough and that we would have perfect biscuits from now on. To our surprise, the next day we were back to burnt biscuits. She had only accidentally made a good batch!

Our problem was that we did not know how my mother had finally made the good biscuits. We had a wealth of information about burnt biscuits but no information about the oven (temperature and duration), the ingredients, or anything about the activities that made the good biscuits.

For us to increase our knowledge base, we must have a vast knowledge of our product PLUS our process.

(P.S. After putting the First Principle of Process Management into place, my mother became and is a world-class biscuit chef.)

Product or Service Data

When we think of the product, we think of it as being the result of something. Product is a tangible something you can touch, see, or review.

Many times we spend heavy amounts of effort monitoring defects, but when we are talking about defects, we are really discussing the product. The problem with focusing on product characteristics is that once the information arrives, it is history. The product is already there. If we have a defect, we now have waste (unhappy customers, scrap, and rework). The only course of action at this point is dealing with the defective product. The very nature of product analysis is reactionary and reacting to defects is tolerating waste. Product analysis is important from the vantage point of being able to know where we are, but it does not provide any insight as to why the defect occurred — in other words, what we need to do to prevent it from happening again.

Before we can begin any analysis, we need a simple strategy for the definition and documentation of our product or service. When formulating a product definition, keep in mind that the definition must be a simple abstract that defines the result of our efforts. Do not attempt to make it more than that by including things like specifications, goals, targets, and customer's requests. The product definition is a document that each associate will be using to clarify what his end result should be. Simplicity, clarity, and conciseness are critical to an effective product definition.

Since we are describing the product or the result, we must avoid discussing the activities. Let's review: in order to make the distinction between product and process clear, the product is a noun and the process is a verb. In the product definition, we must avoid using verbs and stick to nouns and adjectives about the noun only. This is particularly difficult when dealing with service organizations like customer service, communications, or maintenance. Service organizations have a less tangible product, and so the product definition step is the most critical.

The tool that will be used for product definition is called a dependency diagram. The dependency diagram will be used to describe process steps, dependencies, metrics, measurements, goals, and specifications.

Our first effort is to clearly define the product and record that information on the form.

Steps to defining the product

1. Discuss with your associates what the product is.

2. Draft the product definition.

    a) Attempt to limit the definition to one paragraph.

    b) Use nouns and adjectives to describe the product.

    c) Do not use any buzzwords or acronyms as part of the product definition. (This is always a challenge.)

    d) Do not include specifications, service levels, service level agreements, or goals in the product definition.

3. Write the final product definition on a blank sheet of paper. Confer with others to assure that you have a clear, concise document. Once you reach an agreement, write the product definition.

What Are Biscuits Anyway?

Following the previous steps, my grandmother began to describe and define biscuits as flaky, light, round bread. The form below has been completed by my grandmother to describe for future generations what a southern biscuit should be. We use a general description so that over time our product definition will still be valid.

1	Product Definition	- Use Clear, Succinct Paragraphs - Do Not Use Buzzwords or Acronyms - Use Nouns - Do Not Include Specs or Goals

Biscuits:

Flaky, Light, Round Bread

For all products, a clear and concise definition is mandatory. In order for any improvement to take place, the product definition is vital. Even if products are not tangible (i.e. service industry, customer service, maintenance, or distribution), no improvements will occur without clear product definitions.

What Does the Boss Mean When He Asks for a Burnt Biscuit Report?

What is a Burnt Biscuit? A burnt biscuit is a biscuit that does not meet the family's expectations. A burnt biscuit is a defective product. Most people think of a defect as a product with dimensions that fall outside tolerance. By reading the definition, we see that the defect definition includes the imperfect and deficient. Even when we are within specifications, we still have the risk of not meeting the intended purpose.

What the Boss Means! Confusion abounds about the true meaning of what the boss is asking us to do when he requests a burnt biscuit report. This same confusion also occurs when management interprets customer complaints. When the boss or the customer complains about a burnt biscuit (defective product), what they are actually telling us is, *"Make some of Grandma's biscuits and make the burnt biscuits go away"*.

Management and customers express this desire for Grandma's biscuits with a variety of statements such as *"Get me some reports on the number of burnt biscuits"* or *"How many customer complaints have we had this month?"*

Examples of incorrect responses to these statements would be like the following:

- To prepare reams of reports that clearly and vividly describe the number and description of the burnt biscuits. Management asked for the burnt biscuit reports, so they obviously know what they need.

- To hire more quality inspectors to assure that no burnt biscuits reach our customers.

- To prepare a battery of reports describing who is complaining and what they are complaining about.

The Correct Response: By focusing on what the customer wants (Southern biscuits), we may fail to achieve the customer's goal. To provide the customer with Southern biscuits, we must focus on things that the customer will not see. The oven, how it works, temperature, and baking time are not important to the customer. However, these things must be our focus in order to make Grandma's biscuits. Often, management gives mixed signals because it asks for reams and reams of reports about the burnt biscuits. When management asks for these reports, we must be astute enough to realize that what management really wants is Grandma's biscuits all the time. We should provide the management with burnt biscuit reports because they asked for them, but we also need to compile customer surveys to better understand the needs of the customer; oven reports (because we must learn how to make Grandma's biscuits); and, most importantly, a steady stream of perfect biscuits. Both our boss and our customer want a steady stream of perfect southern biscuits. They both want us to make the burnt biscuits go away forever.

What defects do not tell us: If we measure only when we have defective products, we don't get insight into close calls, and how far removed we are from the real target. We are simply measuring our level of incompetence above the customer's incompetence index (specification or SLAs). For us to truly understand our product, we must measure much, much more than defects information.

Many people feel comfortable when they have a product inside the specifications because this means they are having no defects. The problem is that the specifications frequently are the customer's incompetence index, so the customer can be receiving a product inside the specification and still be unhappy.

Many opportunities for improvement pass us by when we only observe defects.

The Importance of Process Data: When we monitor only the product, we are aware only of its deterioration or improvement. This awareness of the change of the product does not give us a reason for the change.

Thus, product monitoring is important, but it

- Is reactionary
- Tolerates waste with no understanding of why

■   Accepts improvement with no understanding of why

Without knowledge of "why," we cannot improve. For us to make Grandma's biscuits, we must understand why things occur the way they do. Product information gives no insight into why we made good biscuits or why we burnt the biscuits. Since we don't know why we are making good biscuits, we cannot repeat the activities that produced them. This loss of knowledge is tragic.

When we monitor the process and the product, the process parameters allow us to know the conditions that caused the change. Monitoring both the product and the process is essential to proactive decisions, improvements, elimination of waste, and understanding the "why's" of change.

Knowledge of "why" allows us to improve continuously. By adding knowledge about the activities required to make a biscuit (process or oven), we begin to learn what is required to make good biscuits. The additional information about the different processes that were used for good biscuits and defective biscuits allows us to continue to repeat the improvements and to discontinue the defects.

In the perfect world of my grandmother and her biscuits, I never saw her check the biscuits when she removed them from the oven. She kept her focus on the process. Since she knew all the subtleties of baking, she would take corrective action as the oven was cooking the biscuits so that, in a proactive manner, she avoided ever making any burnt biscuits. She was a perfect chef; unfortunately, most of us are not perfect chefs of our processes.

Since we live in a not-so-perfect world, and our knowledge of our process is not nearly so complete as my grandmother's was about her oven, we must continue to monitor both our biscuits and our oven with equal intensity. More precisely, we must monitor **both** process and product.

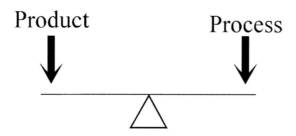

As we gather data and knowledge, we must accumulate equal amounts of knowledge about both the product and the process. This will allow us to build a knowledge base for both the product and the process.

Process Data

A clear understanding of the Principles of Process Management is mandatory to everything we will do. The First Principle states that the underlying component for improving the product is the process. Obviously, we must focus our attention on the process, and our knowledge of it must continue to increase. This expanded knowledge requires clear techniques that will be described in this section. Grandma told me the only way to learn how to make biscuits was to get into the kitchen and learn about the oven. Similarly, to improve our product, we *must* understand our process and this understanding must be converted into a process knowledge base that we can use to improve our product.

This use is called product and process capability. Remember, we have to use our process knowledge base if we want to improve! Increased analysis of the product does not equate to increased knowledge of the process. Knowledge of the process and product are two separate but equal efforts and results. Knowledge of both the product and the process leads to improvements.

Another step to improvement is a clear definition of a process. For our purposes the process (activities to make a product) is made up of four fundamental points:

- Method

- Linear sequence of events
- Time
- Resources

Process management is the judicious use of each of these. It is essential to know when any one of the points changes. When that occurs, we must step back, evaluate the impact, and make a decision as to what steps to follow.

When we think of the process, it is an activity that results in something; it is a verb. We need to focus on the process as the activity is occurring so that we can avoid any problems. Process allows us to be proactive and avoid waste. Simplicity, clarity, and conciseness are critical to an effective process statement.

Since we are describing the process or the activity that generates the result (product), we must avoid discussing the product. Let's briefly review: to make the distinction between product and process vivid, the product is a noun and the process is a verb. In the process definition, we must avoid using nouns and stick to only verbs and adverbs about the verb.

The dependency diagram will be our tool for the process definition. Our next effort is to define the process and record that information on the form. Process definition is much like our earlier discussion about product definition.

Steps to defining the process

1. Discuss with your associates what the process actually is.

2. Draft the process definition.

   a) Attempt to keep the definition to one paragraph.

   b) Use verbs and adverbs to describe the process.

   c) Do not use any buzzwords or acronyms as part of the process definition. (This is always a challenge).

   d) Do not include targets in the process definition.

3. Write the final process definition for each process on a blank sheet of paper. Confer with others to assure that you have a clear, concise document. Once you reach an agreement on each process, write the process definitions on the Walkabout® form.

So How Do We Make Biscuits?

For each process, we need a clear and concise definition of the activities that are included during each step of production. The definition provides the focus for what the activity is designed to accomplish.

With regard to my grandmother's biscuits, we must first list the activities. The process activities are a) mixing and b) baking. Next, we should describe each activity. Mixing is the addition of proper amounts of ingredients so that they can be combined and cut into dough. Baking involves heating the cut dough for a set duration to produce completed biscuits. This information provides a base for us to begin describing how the components and activities work together.

Summary

It should now be clear how important the First Principle of Process Management is. The two broad areas are product and process. In general, it helps to have data from each area.

We now have techniques for documenting the product and process using a dependency diagram. This diagram provides the structure so that we will never skip a step or forget a component. The first step is to define and document the product. The second step is to define and document each process step. A copy of the Walkabout® Dependency Diagram is available for free at www.effectivecallcenters.com.

Chapter Six:

What Can I Manage?

Earlier we discussed the need to understand the First Principle of Process Management. You can't be a great baker like Grandma by sitting in the dining room and eating her biscuits. You can't make Grandma's biscuits by analyzing burnt biscuits. You can't bake Grandma's biscuits by adjusting the oven after each batch of burnt biscuits. You can't manage a bakery by making adjustments and decisions based on the last batch of burnt biscuits. Let's take my Grandma's example and talk about what you can manage in a call center, support center, or help desk.

Let's clarify the word manage. The definition of the word **manage** is *exerting control over.* A person can run an operation reacting to the problems of the day, but this is not managing—it is simply reacting.

To run a call center optimally, we must understand the First Principle of Process Management. Clearly understanding this principle is mandatory to everything we will do. The First Principle of Process Management states *a fundamental understanding of BOTH the product and process is essential to improvement. Both the product and the process must be described and understood individually and separately. **The underlying component for improving the product is the process.***

The First Principle's final sentence is the key. Often all our efforts and energies are directed at analyzing the product. As an example, eating a lot of biscuits does nothing to the baking effort. Having the ability to differentiate between good and bad biscuits does not make you a fine baker. A baker must focus his attention on the baking process. The temperature of the oven, how long the biscuits are in the oven, the location of the baking tray, etc. are the key components for the baker. These are the measures of the process; for the tactician, they are significantly more important than eating the biscuits!

Much discussion is made of monitoring dropped calls. Monitoring dropped calls is interesting, but in a call center monitoring dropped calls does not help us know how to stop dropped calls. The reason most dropped calls occur is because the caller's wait time is too long. But, without adding queuing science, we can't manage wait time, so what are the process issues that drive wait time? Queuing science shows us that wait time is a function of processing time average, processing time variability, and utilization. We can exert control over call processing time central tendency, variability, and agent utilization. Now we have identified what we can manage. These are critical to managing an effective call center. To manage them we must have process metrics of call processing time central tendency, variability, and agent utilization.

Obviously, the person running the call center must focus their attention on the process, and their knowledge of it must continue to increase. My Grandma told me the only way to learn how to make biscuits was to get into the kitchen and learn about the oven. Similarly, to improve our product, we must understand our process, and this understanding must be converted into a process knowledge base that we can use to improve our product. The only way to get this knowledge is through metrics.

The Importance of Process Data

When we just monitor a product metric (like dropped calls), we are aware of its deterioration or improvement only. We might be aware of the change but we do not have a reason for it. Product monitoring is important, but it is reactionary, tolerates waste with no understanding of why, and accepts improvement with no understanding of why.

Without understanding "why" we cannot operate our call center to its maximum performance. For us to make Grandma's biscuits, we must understand why things occur the way they do. Product information gives no insight into why we made good biscuits or why we burnt the biscuits. Since we don't know why we are making good biscuits, we cannot repeat the activities that produced them. This loss of knowledge is tragic.

When we monitor the process and the product, the process parameters, like agent utilization, allow us to know the conditions that caused the change. Monitoring both the product and the process is essential to proactive decisions, improvements, eliminating waste, reducing cost, and understanding the "whys" of change.

By adding knowledge about the activities required to make a biscuit (process), we begin to learn what is required to make good biscuits. The information about the different processes that were used for good biscuits allows us to continue to repeat the good biscuits. Similarly, the information about the different processes that were used for burnt biscuits allows us to change and stop the burnt biscuits.

In the perfect world of my grandmother and her biscuits, I never saw her check the biscuits when she removed them from the oven. She kept her focus on the process. Since she knew all the subtleties of baking, she would take corrective action as the oven was cooking the biscuits so that, in a proactive manner, she avoided ever making any burnt biscuits. She was a perfect chef; unfortunately, most of us are not perfect chefs of our processes.

Since we live in a not-so-perfect world, and our knowledge of our process is not nearly so complete as my grandmother's was about her oven, we must continue to monitor both our biscuits and our oven with equal intensity. More precisely, we must monitor *both* process and product. In our call center some examples of "product" metrics are dropped calls and the amount of time a customer waits for someone to answer his call. Examples of "process" metrics are incoming call volume, average call processing time, call processing time variability, and agent utilization. Monitoring process metrics like agent utilization allows us to become proactive managers.

As we gather data, we must accumulate equal amounts of knowledge about the product *and* the process. This will allow us to build a knowledge base for both.

Increased analysis of the product does not equate to increased knowledge of the process. Knowledge of the process and product are two separate but equal efforts and results. Both product and process knowledge is necessary for improvements.

For our example I will use a center that provides technical support for a point of sale (POS) software product that is sold to retail stores. The center provides technical support and problem resolution to clients who have purchased the company's point of sale software. Since our clients may be in the middle of a transaction with their own customer, the center's rapid response is critical. This center functions as one of the company's storefronts. We want every call to end with a happy and satisfied caller so our clients will continue to buy our products.

Dropped Calls

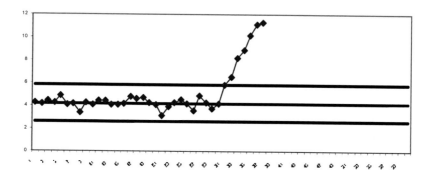

The chart above shows the center's number of dropped calls occurring each day.

If we focus on a product metric like the number of dropped calls, by the time we realize that a shift has occurred we really have a crisis on our hands. We are in damage control mode, fighting fires, and reacting to the problem of the day. Nothing proactive can happen. To make matters worse, we have no way of determining the cause of the dropped calls.

Since our center is a storefront, we want to assure that we keep the dropped calls to a minimum. The main reason that callers drop is because they have grown impatient with our excessive wait time. Below we have defined our process on the metric blueprint for the center.

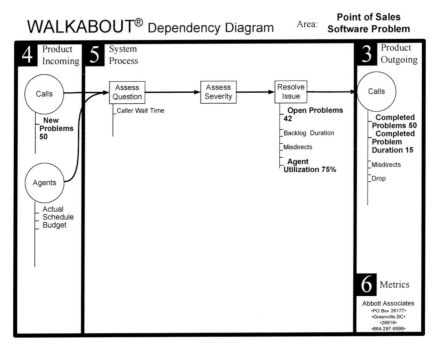

WALKABOUT® Dependency Diagram   Area: **Point of Sales Software Problem**

Think about the product metric of dropped calls as a burnt biscuit report. *Why* do callers drop? The typical reason is excessive wait time. A second metric, and a better metric, would be to track the call wait time.

The tactical view below shows the wait increasing. As the wait time increases we would expect our number of dropped calls to increase. If we look at both the wait time metric and the dropped call metric, we see these two metrics track together. In other words, as the wait time increases, the number of dropped calls increases. Also, as the wait time drops, the number of dropped calls falls.

Wait Time

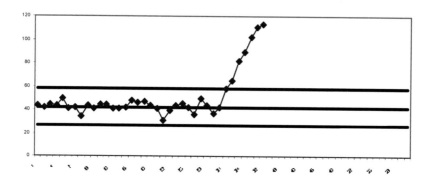

This wait time and dropped call relationship is helpful and interesting, but unless we add science, we cannot manage either dropped calls or wait time. We must have a comprehensive understanding of queuing science, the metric blueprint, and metrics. With this understanding we know what we can manage and what impact the metric has. We have a true cause and effect understanding of the call center.

Total Picture

We will use all the metrics plus the Walkabout® below to find the cause. From queuing science, we know that wait time is a function of agent utilization, processing time average, and the processing time variability. The chart below shows the metric blueprint, process, and tactical metric view. The metric views that are shown are wait time, incoming calls, and average processing time. An actual metric dashboard would show all the metrics, but this is enough to explain the concept.

Wait time could increase because our calls are taking longer or because we have a large volume of incoming calls.

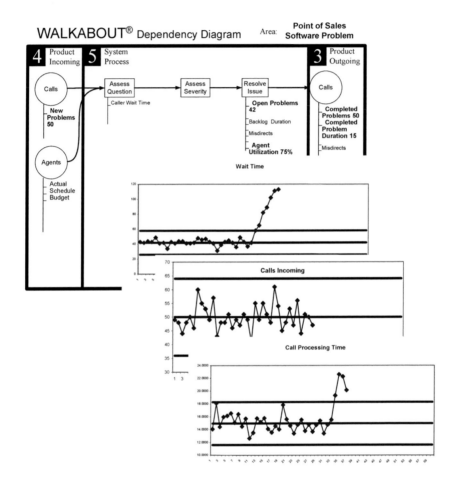

Our metrics show the wait time has increased because the average call processing time has increased. The call volume has remained consistent. With this knowledge we can make a decision regarding a course of action. Some of the actions could be to increase the staff to compensate for the extra time, allow the waits to remain long, and so on.

We can manage center process metrics of utilization, average processing time, and variability of processing time. The utilization is managed by adding, reducing, and redeploying our agents in the center. The processing time average can be managed be changing the script the agents use. The processing time variability can be managed by opening and closing express lanes.

The managing of the center process metrics like utilization, processing time average, and processing time variability is proactive, while product metrics like dropped calls drives a very reactionary style. We can't manage by reaction, but we can manage the process drivers.

Chapter Seven:

Call Centers and Decision-making

Call Center Types

The call center is the storefront for the enterprise. All call centers are classified into two financial types. One is revenue generating, and the other is a cost center. The table below describes both of these types. The revenue financial type sells the company's products and services so the company can make a profit. The cost financial type provides a service but with no payment or compensation and thus reduces profits.

Call Center Financial Types	
Financial Types	**Descriptions**
Revenue	The mission is to sell our products or services and generate as much revenue as possible.
Cost	The mission is to service the customers' or users' needs while no compensation is offered.

Call centers are also classified into five operational types. These types are routing, notification, call management, processing, and content dissemination.

- A routing center transfers a caller to the correct party.

- A notification center notifies the receiver of calls, and the notification may be at a later time. Routing centers make contact immediately, while notification centers have a delay.

- A call management center manages the call from receipt to resolution. This type tracks and documents every step that is done to the request.

- A processing center acts on a request. The businesses using this service include sales, order taking, billing, and computer setup.

- A content dissemination center gives advice and shares information over the telephone or via other methods of contact.

The financial and operational classifications will help us understand why the different types must be managed to support their objectives and values. To achieve production and quality, we must meet the three quality objectives:

- Wait time
- Cost
- Performance

We must marshal our efforts to achieve the target goal. Understanding which type of financial center we are dealing with—revenue or cost—affects how we should manage the center.

Production is often mistakenly defined as keeping all agents busy, getting callers off the lines, or the number of calls handled. The only correct time to count production is when we answer the customer question perfectly, he pays us, and he is happy. The only answer to the question *Do you want quality or quantity?* is that we want *both* quantity *and* quality.

Queuing science allows us to have it all - performance, time, and cost. The issues that allow us to have it all are the utilization, processing time average, and variability. *The Executive Guide to Call Center Metrics* explains the details of the science behind effective call centers, queues, express lanes, and lane balancing. The closer the processing times are to each other, the lower the wait time. The monitor of the spread of the call times is called variability. Standard deviation is a measure of variability. The closer the variability—monitored by standard deviation—is to zero, the less difference in our wait times, and the more opportunity we have to reduce cost.

Effective Operations

In the second decade of the twentieth century when our first call centers were built (telephone operators or a routing center type), all calls into the center were roughly the same duration. Today's world has five operational call center types and two financial types. Science and engineering allow us to design an effective call center and to form call center express lanes. These call center express lanes keep our wait times down, reduce our cost, and provide better performance in our responses to our customers or users.

In my experience I have found a consistent pattern that separates poor, average, and effective operations. There are four traits that can always be found in an effective operation. Trait one is the ability to respond to rapid change. Trait two is a factored organizational structure (express lanes) supported by defined processes. Trait three is a competent workforce that brilliantly executes the business plan. Trait four is optimum decision-making based on proper information. We also have a pattern for the managers of these effective operations.

Managing an Effective Operation

Now, what exactly do call center managers do? There are many functions that are a call center manager's responsibility. These issues include personnel, facility, operations, finance, company and governmental regulation, and planning to name a few. All areas are important, but some cannot be delegated and must be the prime focus of the call center manager.

The one component that is always present in effective operations is that the call center operation managers focus their energy on four key areas. These key areas are a subset of all the call center manager's functions. Brilliant call center managers are better at:

- Understanding their operation.

- Defining and identifying everyone's roles and responsibilities.

- Assessing the operation for correctness, consistency, and capability *on a daily basis*.

- Communicating their expectations to the management team so that the team can execute their roles and responsibilities to support the call center manager's goals.

How do you master these skills? When effective call center managers understand the operation, they define everyone's responsibilities, communicate them to each team member, and have a medium for checking their compliance.

My profession (engineering), corporate America, and my generation have the naïve impression that new equipment and technology will single-handedly win the global productivity battles. The typical firm spends their capital dollars on the newest and finest technology in the world. The initial successes are met with jubilation. After a short period, however, the knowledge of how to maximize the running of the new equipment and technology begins to fade, and our productivity is back where we started, or there are only minor improvements, or, worst yet, things get worse.

A leading company, by contrast, is not only investing in hardware and technology, but also in the knowledge of better ways to run the center. A scientifically designed process that everyone understands is the platform for an effective center and continued improvement.

To this end, there are three Principles of Process Management for running an effective call center. They will assist us to rapidly and proactively respond to the ever-changing business world so that we always have an effective center. These principles are the First Principle of Product and Process, the Second Principle of Division of Labor, and the Third Principle of Walkabout® base-camp. This chapter will focus on developing the second principle, decision making.

Decision-making and the Wisdom of the Second Principle

The **Second Principle of Process Management** states that *Division of Labor is the framework for all aspects of decision-making. It must be clearly understood to separate the policy, strategic, and tactical decisions. Operations makes the tactical decisions of running the facility. Management makes the strategic decisions of assessing the facility's suitability for the job. Executives make the policy decisions of providing the vision for the business.*

Decision-making is defined as reaching a conclusion. For our purposes, the definition must be broadened. We will define a **decision** as *reaching a conclusion plus the execution of the decision.* Just having a good idea or knowing how to fix a problem is not enough. To say that we have made a decision, we must bring the concept, idea, or solution to completion.

There is a historical foundation for the Second Principle of Process Management. In the late 1700s, in his book *The Wealth of Nations*, Adam Smith coined the term **Division of Labor** to explain specialization of manual labor. The second principle expands that concept into the realm of decision-making. Since decision-making is the heart and soul of effective organizations, the second principle is crucial for far-reaching success.

Division of Labor drives the decision-making process. It dictates who will be in charge of the different kinds of decisions (policies, strategies, or tactics). We are doomed to failure if we do not grasp, use, and communicate the Division of Labor.

Policies provide the vision to guide the organization. Executives must develop and define this vision. Good decisions can be made only when a clear understanding of the purpose and need are known. This information must be communicated to all the decision-makers. A clear mission or objective will provide the direction for the course that we must plot.

For effective change, we must have a clear idea of our direction. A stated vision serves in three ways: purpose, feasibility, and baseline. A vision helps keep the problem in clear mental focus as we dive into details.

The vision is a statement that summarizes the goals of the business in terms of **performance** (*What* is to be done?), **time** (*When* must it be done?), and **cost** (*How much* will it cost?). A good solution must specifically address the three critical factors: performance, time, and cost.

Keep in mind there is typically no one solution that will be perfect. We must weigh performance, time, and cost to pick the optimum solution.

Strategists provide the facility to meet the policy vision. This vision must be communicated so that the strategists can build a facility that supports the policy vision. Capability is a major strategic issue associated with management, customer, and sales concerns.

Tactics are defined as accomplishing the goal using available means. Control is a major tactical issue associated with operational duties. Operations makes the tactical decisions of running the facility the strategist provides.

Tactical execution is required for strategic decisions to be effective. If operations fails to correctly run the facility, no strategy will work. Our strategic decision-makers must count on our tactical decision-makers to do their job, for only then can the strategic decisions be effective. Many strategic options are available, but they will work only if the operation runs smoothly.

Responsibility

Division of Labor is the driving force for decision responsibility. Division of Labor dictates who will be in charge of the different kinds of decisions (policy, strategic, or tactical). A clear appreciation of whether the decision is policy, strategic, or tactical must be clear because the decision options may change according to our decision type. In other words, a policy or strategic or tactical view of the same problem may result in different decision options.

Let's go over an example of decision options based on responsibility. Since most people have flown on commercial airliners, let's analyze some potential airline industry problems and decisions.

Our first situation involves deciding whether or not to let an aircraft depart. We encounter two different situations in which the aircraft is not completely up to speed.

- A mechanic finds a tire that is flat. The mechanic would be correct in not letting the plane fly with the flat tire because that action could jeopardize the lives of the people on the plane. This would be a tactical decision and totally correct.

- A flight attendant finds a tray table that will not stay in the upright position. This is not a threat to the safety of the plane. As a stop gap measure, the attendant might choose to tape the tray up until the flight arrives at a destination where the tray table can be fixed. This decision is also a correct tactical decision.

Our second situation involves the capacity of the aircraft fleet. The flight that we are analyzing is completely full. All rows in the coach cabin seat three passengers abreast, and each seat is occupied. One passenger violently complains because he is seated in the center of three seats. His legs are cramped due to the lack of legroom.

- The flight attendant might not allow the plane to fly. In an attempt to be customer driven, he might reduce the number of passengers so that the complaining passenger could have more room. This is an example of a tactician inadvertently trying to make a decision that must be made by a strategist. Tacticians should not make strategic decisions. Instead, they must execute the strategic decisions.

- Management must assume its strategic role. If enough customers are complaining, management must assess the number of passengers per flight. Strategically, we are choosing the resources and how they will be used. Management must decide whether it can effectively operate at a profit with fewer passengers. Another consideration is whether the airline will charge a higher fare if it chooses to reduce the number of passengers on board each flight.

These types of decisions are everyday occurrences and must be made by the correct player.

Our third situation is the everyday question of how we connect a caller to the right agent. Many executives improperly abdicate this decision to the technical staff. This example is a reservation center for a very upscale resort. Our rooms start at $500 per night and range up to $2,000 per night.

- Our policy maker might abdicate his role to the technician who programs the automated call director. The technician programs the system to force our (high revenue) customers to use their phone keypad to enter most of the information required to make the reservation. The technician proudly announces how much money is being saved by his efforts. This has really become a self-service operation. Rather than saving money we are making our customers do the work. We have transferred the cost from us to our customer, which is neither good nor bad but must be a policy decision as to how we will treat our customers. This is an example of a tactician inadvertently trying to make a decision that must be made by policy and strategic decision-makers.

- The second option has the policy maker providing a clear vision of our business. This vision reflects our resort, our customers, the room rate price point of above $500 per night, and our business. This vision is to make our customer experience splendid service from making a reservation to checkout and everything in between. Our vision for reservations is for our agent to handle every detail of the stay, including the reservation itself. To make the customer's initial experience stellar every call must be answered — by a human — within 30 seconds of the first ring.

This example shows the importance of a policy vision. The strategist must build a facility that supports the policy vision. The tactician must run the strategically provided facility as correctly and consistently as possible.

Strategic decisions must be continually validated to assure that the plan is still appropriate. The assumptions of the plan or the conditions may change such that a new strategy is required.

Accountability

What not to do is just as important as what to do. Second principle violations must be understood and avoided in order to make effective decisions. The harder a decision maker works with improper instructions (violating the second principle), the poorer the performance. Quality will degenerate. As an example, when an operation violates the Second Principle on an extremely capable process, we will make the process appear less capable than it really is. Instead, we must run the process to its own personality, as correctly and consistently as possible.

For us to be able to properly lead, we must know which things are within an individual's scope of influence. All decisions are marked by discipline and perseverance, and all decisions require risk. When we are making business decisions, we must strive to minimize our risk of a bad decision.

There is a distinct difference between policy versus strategic versus tactical accountability. We know that Division of Labor is key to decision making. Without this understanding, policy, tactical, and strategic decisions become cloudy. This clouded understanding will make any decision process impossible because we may be doing more harm than good. The Second Principle of Process Management's Division of Labor allows us to determine who should be held accountable.

Scope of influence is critical. Clarity of decision type — an operational or management /sales/customer issue — drives whether we are considering

89

a policy or a tactical or a strategic decision. The Division of Labor drives the options essential to all decisions.

The following table shows us a summary of Division of Labor and the three decision types.

	Executive	Management	Operations
Decisions	Policy	Strategic	Tactical
Accountability	Matching our products to customer's need	Finding customers who will buy our products	The correct and consistent running of the facility
Responsibility	Future direction of the business	Providing the facility that will produce what the customer wants	Running the provided facility correctly and consistently
Terms	Vision	Capability	Control
Tools for Decisions	Market research, Financial reports	Strategic views from capability studies, Service Level Agreements	Tactical view from control chart, control limits, targets
Duties	Provide and share the vision	Build a plan and assess the impact of change	Execute the plan and detect change
Functions	Develop a business vision	Provide the resources, time, and place to resolve plan changes	Detect change, Determine cause

Policy Reports

We know that executives make policy decisions. Policy decisions require information, which require the classic financial reports. Below is an example of a policy report of the revenue of the business.

Revenue											
2001											
Jan	Feb	Mar	Apr	May	Jun	Jul	Aug	Sep	Oct	Nov	Dec
$ 404,469	$ 446,624	$ 347,164	$ 329,862	$ 386,716	$ 351,994	$ 373,752	$ 432,657	$ 354,479	$ 324,049	$ 395,372	$ 396,130

These reports are done monthly to show the business' progress. These reports have a month-over-month layout to put the current month into context. These reporting methods work well to support that mission and clearly support the policy decision-making. All reports and metrics must have a clear objective that they support. These policy reports do meet their objective.

Imagine that the center we are running is an order-processing center. The business spends money on direct mail brochures to convince the customers to buy their products. The call center is the storefront for our business, the place where all revenue comes in.

Since executives are used to seeing these policy reports, they assume that the same format will work for strategic call center reports. We prepare reports that look like the ones below using the policy format. We monitor the abandonment rate, or dropped calls, for our center. We are also monitoring the percent of calls that fall below the SLA of a 20-second pickup time.

	Phone Metrics											
	2001											
	Jan	Feb	Mar	Apr	May	Jun	Jul	Aug	Sep	Oct	Nov	Dec
Abandonment	1.5%	0.7%	1.7%	0.6%	0.7%	0.8%	0.9%	1.1%	1.4%	0.7%	1.6%	1.8%
Answer within 20 sec	88%	95%	84%	96%	94%	93%	88%	89%	89%	92%	89%	86%

We add some graphics to the report and begin to feel that our reporting is good. The call center is the revenue base, and each customer is a value. Because of our direct mail cost and the potential revenue each call brings to the company, a single dropped call is too many.

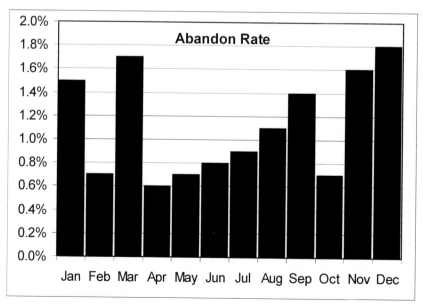

Let's look in more detail to see what happened in the last month on the graph, the month of December. The chart below is a daily look at the abandonment rate. This chart displays the percent of people that got so frustrated that they hung up before we could take their order. The monthly report shows a bad sign but when we look at each day we see several spikes that are much worse. These peaks and valleys could not be seen in the monthly look.

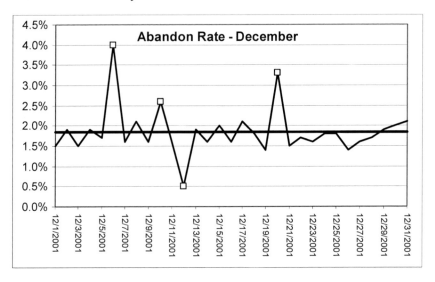

Our strategic responsibilities are to provide the facility and to assist in running the center. Our strategic call center decision-maker cannot use this monthly report to support those missions because the information is not timely. We need to assess and change the call center facility in an almost real-time manner. Even looking at the daily report we have no information as to what to do. The reports are well intended, but, as the saying goes, the road to hell is paved with good intentions.

We need timely information that answers many questions. How will we know how to stop the dropped calls? How will we know what the cause of the dropped calls is?

Financial reports are great, but operational management requires more details and quicker response. To support these operational needs more tools are required. These tools start with operational budgets, capital budgets, and cost transactional systems, to name a few.

Strategy and tactics must work and grow together. As the facilities grow and change, we must communicate these strategic changes to our tactical workforce. Should our tactics remain stagnant or unchanging, horrendous consequences will abound. We must continually evaluate our decisions and the premises around which they are based.

Strategic decisions demand a vast and internalized knowledge capability. Each individual must make the knowledge capability an internal component of all his decisions and thought processes. Strategies must be bold, rapid, and revolutionary. Tactical decisions also demand a vast knowledge of capability, but they still require a good strategic base. Tactical decisions are methodical, procedural, and evolutionary.

Where Do I Fit in the Decision-making Process?

Many times I am asked, *What kind of decision am I making? Am I part of management or operations? Am I strategic or tactical?* These questions are vital to understanding the correct course of action.

A private in the army is obviously a tactical individual. The private's goal is to efficiently and correctly execute the plan. The private's goal and mission is clear. In contrast, a general in the army is obviously a strategic individual. The general's goal is to provide a plan that will meet the political and military objective. The general's goal and mission is also clear. The roles of the private and the general are both clear with no ambiguity.

The business "general" is the president or CEO. The president's objective is to provide a corporate policy or vision. The president, like the general, has a clear role of strategic leadership and decision-making. The business "private" is the center's agent. The agent's role is to properly follow the provided script. The agent's mission is clearly tactical.

The army has many levels between the private and the general. Sergeants, lieutenants, captains, majors, colonels, and more fall between the general and the private. These decision-maker levels are equivalent to business middle managers. Each level is conducting some amount of strategic and tactical decision-making. Middle level managers are continuously swapping the general's decision-making hat and the private's decision-making hat.

Swapping from strategic to tactical is the difficult part of decision-making. Each individual must grasp the importance of this ongoing change in decision-making roles. The critical issue is whether the decision that we are making is tactical or strategic. We must be flexible enough to understand our decision-making position.

Decision-making Options

We have discussed an operational philosophy based on change management. This is built around decision-making when changes are small. The following will act as an introduction to the kinds of decisions made in call centers.

In the 1950s and 1960s Mayberry TV series, many truths and morals were described. When trouble was beginning, Barney Fife would go to Sheriff Taylor and discuss the potentially bad situation. In Barney's zeal and excitement to avoid trouble, he would say in a very excited tone, "Andy, we've got to Nip it, Nip it, Nip it in the Bud."

In many ways, Barney was a forerunner to effective decision-making. Changes need to be deliberate and with a steady hand. When a change is detected, the reason for the change must be determined. Its impact must be evaluated to assess improvement or deterioration. A rapid response is required. The responses will be determined based on the cause and the impact to the customer. Improvements will be replicated; deterioration will be removed.

The idea of effective decisions could create a Barney Fife School of Management. The watchword would be the "Nip it in the Bud" philosophy. This could allow us to more fully understand what is happening, why it is happening, and what the impact is.

If we make our decisions when things are small, we will avoid big problems and the crisis that comes from them. The big problems and chaos makes the decisions huge. This can go a long way to avoiding the pitfalls of having to decide on the best of bad decisions.

The moral of the story is like Mayberry — we have to build our call center to give us good options in our decision-making. No matter how good our decision-making, we must be in a position of having good options.

Any decision will be marked by risk. No decision, i.e. doing nothing at all, is still a decision. Risk must not be confused with recklessness. Our job is to minimize our risk. We want to be able to make our decision when the choices are good ones. We also want to make our decisions early, so the impact will be small and the consequences of a bad decision will also be small.

Typical Call Center Decisions

Call center personnel typically make either strategic or tactical decisions. Let's take a more in-depth look at them. Tactics are defined as accomplishing the goal using available means. Control is the major tactical issue associated with operational duties. Operations — the supervisors and agents — make the tactical decisions of running the provided facility.

The strategist must provide this facility. A call center facility is made up of physical and intellectual tools. The physical tools are the computers, phone systems, IVR and call directors, etc. The intellectual tools are the knowledge, science, and metrics of how to run the center. Training for both tool types is required. Capability is the major strategic issue associated with management, customer, and sales concerns. The strategist must provide a capable facility for the tactical workforce.

Tactical execution is required for strategic decisions to be effective. If operations fails to correctly run the facility, no strategy will work. The strategic decision-makers must count on the tactical decision-makers to do their job, for only then can the strategic decisions be effective. Many strategic options are available, but they will work only if the operation runs smoothly.

What not to do is just as important as what to do. Second Principle violations must be understood and avoided in order to effectively make decisions. The Good Trooper Award is given to the supervisor who tries to take the responsibility for strategic decisions. The harder a supervisor works with improper instructions (violating the Second Principle), the poorer the call center results. Quality will continue to degenerate. The better and more conscientious the employee, the worse the situation will become because the person will go to any lengths to carry out those improper directions.

Chapter Seven

When operations violates the Second Principle on an extremely capable process, the call center will appear less capable than it really is. Instead, we must run the call center to its own personality, as correctly and consistently as possible. We must not be lulled into accepting services that are only as good as the customer tolerates and allow the process to float below the SLA.

Tactical Roles

Running the call center is clearly tactical and the job of the tactical decision-maker. These tactical decisions are:

- Noting when a change in the process and product metrics has occurred.

- Alerting management when a change has occurred so that the strategic decision-maker can assess the impact of the change on the product or the process.

- Finding the cause of a change.

- Working with the strategic decision-maker in deciding what action to take.

- Having the process knowledge to know when and what adjustments are required.

Strategic Roles

Peak efficiency is dependent on the strategist providing a correct and capable facility. Our tactical work force must count on the strategic players to deliver their end of the bargain.

Providing the call center facility is clearly strategic and the job of the strategic decision-maker. These strategic decisions are:

- Providing the tools, methods, structure, and technology to meet the policy vision of the executive.

- Assessing the impact on the customer or user when a change in the process and product metrics has occurred.

- Dynamically retooling the center to meet business changes.

Since strategy and tactics are very different, a different metric view for each seems logical. The tactical view supports the need to detect a change. The strategic view supports the assessment of how well the center is performing, as a function of the customer's needs.

Policy Roles

Peak efficiency requires a clear vision with the strategist providing a correct and capable facility. Our tactical work force must count on the strategic players to deliver their end of the bargain.

Providing the business and call center vision is clearly policy and the job of the policy decision-maker. These policy decisions are:

- Providing the policy vision of the business.

- Determining how we will treat our customers.

Since policy, strategy, and tactics are very different, a different view and objective for each seems logical. The tactical view supports the need to detect a change. The strategic view supports the assessment of how well the center is performing, as a function of the customer's needs. The policy view shows how we are meeting the company or business vision.

You Can't Do It Alone

Understanding who is responsible for each task is key to a successful organization. If supervisors try taking on every role, they risk not being successful in any role. Violating the second principle by compounding the responsibilities of management with those of operations leads to chaotic decision-making. The strategic decision-maker can only ask operations to do what the facility is capable of doing. In this way, we can hold operations accountable for correctly and consistently running the call center facility. Management must never abdicate their strategic responsibility to provide a capable facility.

Let's discuss the climate in the southern region of the United States. This will allow me to explain roles and the trust required for an effective team. During a typical summer, a heat wave engulfs the whole South.

Chapter Seven

As a boy growing up in Tennessee, I remember trying to stay cool in church. The local mortuary supplied hand held fans to everyone in our church. Using those fans never kept us cool. Maybe that is why the mortuary was the supplier--they wanted us to know who to call when we passed away from the heat! Motivation, violent hand motion, and rapid bursts could not overcome the lack of a proper tool to keep us cool.

As ineffective as they were, those fans were the best tool at the time. Later, mechanical fans were introduced but the heat still won the battle. Only when air conditioning came along were the hot summer days manageable.

Each of these cooling systems (hand fans, electric fans, and air conditioning) must be run to its maximum potential. Then a fair assessment of each option's efficiency can be made. We expect our strategic decision-makers to continually invent, listen to suggestions, and try new options until ultimately an acceptable solution is devised. This acceptable solution is then built into a capable facility.

Tactical personnel cannot overcome bad strategy, nor can strategic personnel overcome bad tactical execution. When strategic and tactical personnel both do their jobs, they form a team. Operations is in deep trouble when management does not do its decision-making job of providing the facility. If the facility (available means) is not capable, we are doomed to having dissatisfied customers and stockholders. If operations does not perform its role of running the facility (available means) correctly and consistently, then how can management assess the impact to the customer? The proper support information must come together to build a finely honed partnership that allows for good, effective, clear decisions.

When policy, strategic, and tactical personnel do their jobs, they form a team. The proper support information must come together to build a finely honed partnership that allows for good, effective, clear decisions. Operations must count on the executives to provide a clear vision and management to provide a proper facility for the mission. Policy, strategic, and tactical decision-makers must trust that each will step up and take responsibility for the job. Then each can focus their energies on brilliantly executing their decisions, trusting the others will do the same.

Summary

The classic financial reporting methods were designed for the policy maker. The following table shows us a summary of Division of Labor and the three decision types.

	Executive	Management	Operations
Decisions	Policy	Strategic	Tactical
Accountability	Matching our products to customer's need	Finding customers who will buy our products	The correct and consistent running of the facility
Responsibility	Future direction of the business	Providing the facility that will produce what the customer wants	Running the provided facility correctly and consistently
Terms	Vision	Capability	Control
Tools for Decisions	Market research, Financial reports	Strategic views from capability studies, Service Level Agreements	Tactical view from control chart, control limits, targets
Duties	Provide and share the vision	Build a plan and assess the impact of change	Execute the plan and detect change
Functions	Develop a business vision	Provide the resources, time, & place to resolve plan changes	Detect change, Determine cause

Chapter Eight:
Operational Philosophy

Call centers have radically changed from their beginnings in the early 1900s. Now, rather than one simple call center type where everyone does the same thing and every call is about the same length, we have five uniquely different call center types. The five operational call center types—routing, notification, call management, processing, and content dissemination—require specialized tools, methods, technology, and processes. Adding to this complex mix are the two financial center types of revenue and cost.

In the early days of the simple call center, the center's greatest expenses were far and away telephone service charges. These large and complex phone bills drove management to focus only on these telephone charges. Today the science inside the center is more complex because of the many demands from the five different call center types. This requires a conceptual understanding of call center science issues, from express lane determination to lane balancing, plus the original telephony issues. Metrics and sigma play a huge role in the design of an effective call center and the decision-making required to run an optimal call center.

Walkabout® Base-camp

The **Third Principle of Process Management** states *an effective operation must be built on a base of correctness, consistency, and capability. The strategic decision makers provide a correct facility for the tactical decision makers to run correctly. Consistency is the level at which the tactical workforce is able to hit the target. Capability is strategic in nature. It measures the facility's ability to provide what the customer wants.*

Running your call center is like an expedition ascending a mountain to its summit. A mountain climbing expedition always meets roadblocks. The expedition requires certain essential elements to overcome these obstacles and so does running your center. The mountain climbing expedition's essentials include the right equipment, access to the essentials of life (food, water, air), a stable launch point, and properly trained team members. These essentials are referred to as the base-camp for an expedition. In an effective call center, a base-camp will also be required. The operational base-camp's components are correctness,

100

consistency, and capability, which we will refer to as the Walkabout® base-camp.

The following dependency diagram allows us to discuss the first component: correctness. To explain the concept, imagine that we have a small call center with three agents. We have purchased a ticketing system to track our work.

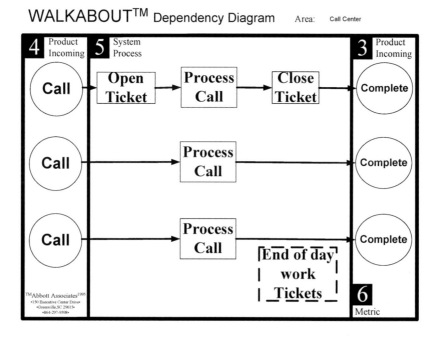

The first agent opens the ticket when the call comes in, processes the call, posts the required information into the system as the call progresses, and at the completion of the call closes the ticket. The second agent feels that using the ticketing system is too much paperwork or in his words is "nonproductive work" so he chooses to never use the system. The third agent processes all the calls and writes the required information on a sheet of paper. Then, at the end of the day, he posts that work into the ticketing system.

If we enlarge this situation to a center with 30 or 100 or 300 agents, we begin to see that we cannot really tell anything about the center. We have no method to see if someone is doing better or worse than anyone else. In other words, there is no correct process and everyone does the best they can. We cannot establish the cost of a call, predict the processing time of a call, or manage the center because everything— every call, every response—is different.

First, the strategic correctness of the six sigma design must be determined. A correct, functional organization with clearly defined roles must be established. A clearly defined product and a detailed method or process must be created. The six sigma design strategic decision-makers must develop and clearly communicate these correct processes. The strategist will provide a Walkabout® schematic diagram of the method. On each metric a target will be provided.

For the center we have been discussing the strategist must first establish a correct method. The strategist decides that whenever a call comes in, a ticket must be opened, then the call will be processed with all information documented during the call, and finally when the call is complete the ticket will be closed. This must be communicated to the tactical workforce.

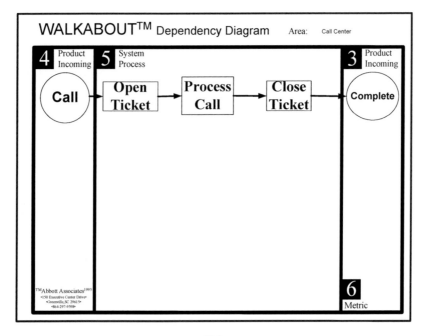

The tactical workforce (our line supervisors and agents) must brilliantly execute the plan, methods, and target settings. Brilliant execution should not be confused with perfection. We, as human beings, will always strive for perfection, but the reality is that it may be outside our grasp. Correctness is the first step toward building the Walkabout® base-camp. This correctness is key for our call center to perform properly.

The second step toward completing the base-camp means monitoring each call center metric. This will determine how consistent each product and process metric is. As tacticians strive for perfection, this consistency provides a way of predicting what will be produced time after time. Each metric must have its own consistency established. This consistency is monitored through the use of tactical mathematical tools called control charts. These are our first view of the metrics. These tactical views must be used for running our provided call center facility.

Finally, the strategic decision-maker is positioned to assess how well the call center meets the customer's expectation. This is the center's capability.

Take special note: Correctly and consistently running the provided call center facility are tactical issues. Capability is a strategic issue. Both the tactician and strategist must work together to achieve the best performance from the center.

With a base camp of a correct, consistent, and capable center, we are now in a position to understand the center. This environment allows us to develop an operational philosophy.

Operational Philosophy

Many techniques for running an operation have been used over the years, with varying degrees of success. The Walkabout® Method uses change management as the overall strategy. In basic terms, this means we hold everything stable. The Walkabout® base-camp provides this stable environment. When a change occurs, we assess the impact.

What is required is an objective means of detecting change and assessing each change's impact on the call center. These assessments must be immediate and real-time. Metrics are the key to this operational philosophy. Metrics are used here to detect change and then to assess the change. Changes that result in deterioration are eliminated. Changes that bring improvements are incorporated into a revised plan for the center.

This next graphic shows the flow of our operational philosophy. Metrics are our eyes and ears for this proactive philosophy. For improvement to occur, change must occur. Any time a change occurs, even in the best of circumstances, the result might be negative. Thus we need a change detector and its companion for assessing every change's impact on the call center's capability; this paints the call center's total picture.

We have developed an improvement model using change management.

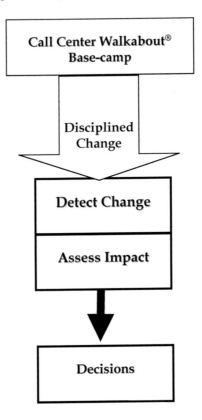

The tactician detects the changes and the strategist assesses the impact to the call center. Use of this new model allows us to dramatically accelerate our improvement, maximize decision-makers' time, reduce wait time, provide better service, and reduce cost in our call center.

Walkabout® Management Style and Effective Managers

Earlier we explained the **Four Traits of an Effective Operation**.

- Trait one is the ability to respond to rapid change.

- Trait two is a factored organizational structure supported by defined processes.

- Trait three is a competent workforce that brilliantly executes the plan.

- Trait four is optimum decision-making based on proper information.

We also listed the **Four Traits of Effective Managers**. Effective managers are better at

- Understanding their operation.

- Defining and identifying everyone's roles and responsibilities.

- Assessing the operation for correctness, consistency, and capability on a daily basis.

- Communicating their expectations to the management team so that the team can execute their roles and responsibilities to support the call center manager's goals.

Using the Walkabout® Method, effective call center managers will rapidly understand their facility inside and out, the operational dependencies, and what the key metrics are.

With this operational philosophy the manager has a medium for doing their daily assessment—the Walkabout®. The daily metrics views are from measured results not the opinion or voice of the staff. Initially every area of the call center is looked at, and as compliance is achieved,

105

the focus shifts to the change management method. With a base-camp and metrics to test the call center, the manager will be assured that the operation is running correctly, consistently, and capably.

Use of this new model allows us to dramatically accelerate our improvement process. From the beginning we have worked to provide tools to help all operational managers be effective. When a call center manager is doing a Walkabout®, he is assessing the center.

Walkabout® and Tactical Views

The tactical view is called a control chart. It is the tool to monitor the metrics' consistency around our target. For every metric we must have a control chart monitoring our actual results. We will monitor all three types of metrics: incoming product, process, and outgoing product. To keep our example simple, I have narrowed our discussion to just one metric. The metric that we will use is the number of calls completed.

The control chart gives us a tactical decision-making tool to determine when any movement in the metric we are measuring is truly a change. First, the call center was engineered for a call volume of 50 calls. We run the call center with this target, gathering and posting the readings. These values will be used to build a time sequence chart.

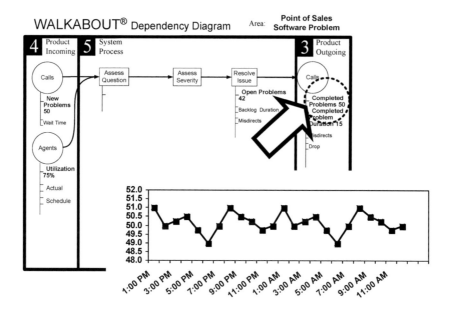

WALKABOUT® Dependency Diagram   Area: Point of Sales Software Problem

Chronological sequence is necessary for identifying causes. By maintaining the integrity of the time sequence, we also have the ability to take care of our time-series grouping and near real-time reporting.

Since our measurement readings are intended to paint a total picture of the call center, they are not just to detect bad service. They must detect change, monitor consistency, and assess impact to the customer. Based on some math done by our strategic analyst, control limits are calculated from the actual results of running the call center to help us determine consistency. The chart below shows the metric with our control limits for detecting change.

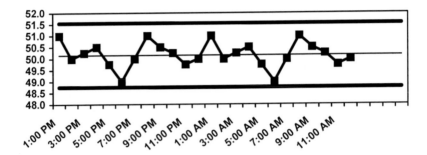

When the metric measurements on the control chart do not violate any of the tactical rules, we can declare our center's metric to be in a state of statistical control. For more details on the tactical rules, read *The Executive Guide to Call Center Metrics*.

By using the Walkabout® to establish that we are running to the target we have now passed the first two milestones in our journey to the Walkabout® base camp. Our strategic decision-makers will tackle the third milestone, which is assessing capability.

The tacticians have kept their end of the bargain. When the center is running correctly and consistently, we are ready for the handoff to the strategist. A true team is built on trust. But we not only trust, we verify. The strategist now takes the measurements and assesses the capability of the center's metrics. This capability shows our actual results compared to the Service Level Agreement (SLA).

The Walkabout® and Strategic Views

The strategist does the capability study by superimposing the actual metric measurements onto the SLA or specification limit. The bar on the capability study below reflects the actual measurements showing the number of occurrences by group. The line is the SLA.

The metric measurements from our study are shown with the SLA or specification limit. When the strategist has charted the capability, an expected zero percent defect rate is determined. As long as the process stays correct and consistent with no changes, then we should continue to never see the call volume exceed our abilities.

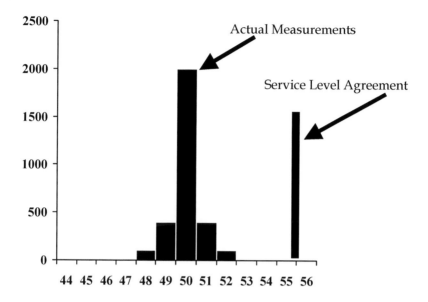

Should you desire to find out the details of strategic and tactical studies, the book *Preparing Call Center Metrics* is available through your local or online bookstore.

Now let's put the Walkabout® operational philosophy and metrics into practice with the example we used earlier of the technical support for our point of sale software product.

Total Picture Working Together

We will use all the metrics plus the Walkabout® below to find the cause of the increased wait times. From queuing science, we know that wait time is a function of agent utilization, processing time average, and the processing time variability. The chart below shows the metric blueprint, process, and tactical metric view. The metric views that are shown are wait time, incoming calls, and average processing time. An actual metric dashboard would show all the metrics, but this is enough to explain the concept.

Wait time could increase because our calls are taking longer or because we have a large volume of incoming calls.

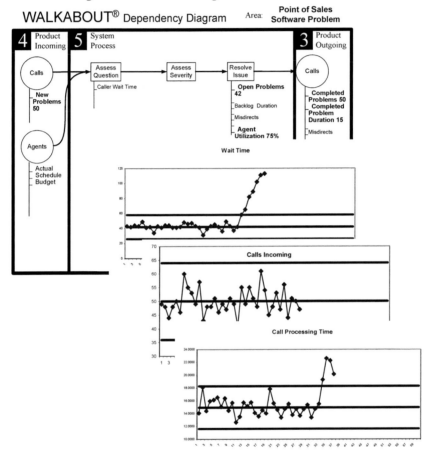

Our metrics show the wait time has increased because the average call processing time has increased. The call volume has remained consistent. With this knowledge we can make a decision regarding a course of action. Some of the actions could be to increase the staff to compensate for the extra time, allow the waits to remain long, and so on.

We religiously monitor each metric for change using our tactical view. As long as no changes occur, no strategic studies are required. When the tactical supervisor detects a change, the supervisor must begin the search for the cause and alert the strategic decision-maker to assess the impact. When the cause is determined and the assessment is done, the decision can be made as to what to do.

When we start investigating the change, we learn that our software developers have notified us of the release of an update the software at the same time the change occurred. This new release of software has many new features that our customers have been asking for. These new features add a new level of complexity to our software. We realize that the updated point of sale software has caused an increase in the call processing time since our agents now need to explain the new features. The time frame of information after the change will be compiled to assess the impact on our center. Our call processing time SLA is still 45 minutes per call.

This chart shows where the call processing time is distributed after the new release of software.

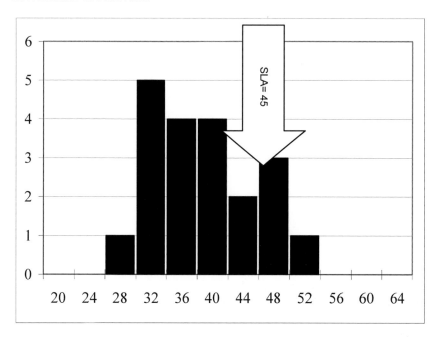

Now we have the total and comprehensive package of tools that allows our workforce to effectively do their role. Let's do a quick review. When a change is detected, the supervisor must do two things. First, a study to determine the cause of the change must be initiated. Second, the supervisor must alert the strategic decision-maker to the change.

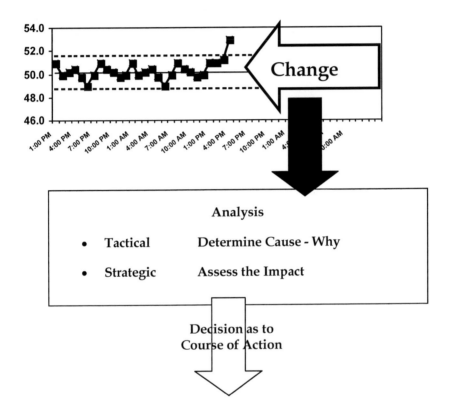

Determining why there was a change is a tactical responsibility. Assessing the impact of the change is a strategic responsibility. The answer to these two questions drives the response to the change. Change must not be confused with defective product or poor service. Change can be either an improving product or service or a deteriorating product or service.

The manager should do a daily assessment using a Walkabout®. The daily metrics views are from measured results not the opinion or voice of the staff. Initially every area of the call center is looked at, and as compliance is achieved, the focus shifts to the change management method. With a base-camp and metrics to test the call center, the manager will be assured that the operation is running correctly, consistently, and capably.

Chapter Nine:

Segmentation

To make a product or provide a service, we must understand the linking and interacting of individual processes that form a system. The system can be a call center, a help desk, a complete manufacturing facility, one manufacturing department, a maintenance organization, a distribution center, a warehousing center, a human relations department, a training department, an order processing department, or the whole enterprise. A **system** is *a series of processes (activities) interacting as a unit, unified whole, or team to effectively produce a product.*

Systems Design

There are several methods for designing, defining, and documenting the systems. Many people use what is called an *As-is Method*. When we use that method we are assuming that the people that did the design used logic and science. Sometimes we don't know where components, issues, products, and so on came from. We must make sure that we can document and prove all the information that is presented. In addition, we must never allow opinions to be presented as facts. All facts must be presented to all parties in a manner that allows them to research, question, and analyze our facts.

The As-is Method is not a bad method for an evolutionary approach. But if we go back and revisit our grocery store checkout, the As-is Method would never discover the concept of express lanes.

A revolutionary technique for improvement is an engineering design. This starts with a clean slate, and applies science to engineer the most effective means of running the operation. As we design any operation science must be the foundation. In an electrical motor plant we must understand Newton's laws, the science of electricity. For our purposes in a call center we must start with a good understanding of queuing science.

The objective of our efforts is to design the system so that we truly have engineered an effective operation. In the case of my grandmother and her biscuits, we must describe the flow of activities or processes that are required to manufacture biscuits. This linking, sequences, and flow of products and processes is critical to understanding the system. If we didn't appreciate the importance of the sequence of steps in making biscuits, we might try to bake the ingredients prior to mixing them. The dependency diagram uses pictures to describe the sequence of the process.

People, processes, and technology are often used to describe the components for a system. For our purposes in an engineering design, the following sequential steps are required:

1. Factoring the business for segmentation
2. Establish a dependency diagram
3. Select the appropriate process method
4. Establish metrics and target settings

Each of these steps is of equal importance. This chapter will deal with step one—factoring the business into segments. This segmentation will allow our determination of express lane candidates.

For a complete discussion of all four steps in sigma call center design, read *Designing Effective Call Centers*.

To understand the reasons for the structure and how to do the segmentation, let's revisit our grocery store example.

Factoring

Earlier, we discussed rethinking the whole grocery store checkout methodology and came to some interesting results. The crude but efficient grocery store has the three clerks fully loaded and always busy. The average wait is ten minutes and the cost is $30,000. The effective grocery store has a new method based on a factored structure. The factoring looks for processing times that are similar. The effective grocery store takes a different approach of balancing both the store's needs and the customer's needs by understanding queuing science and the need to minimize processing time variability. One clerk is processing full buggies and the second clerk is processing one-item customers using an express lane. With this approach the average wait is 9.9 minutes and the cost is $20,000.

The table below compares our crude approach to the factored express lane approach.

	Crude Approach	Express Lane Approach
Number of clerks	3 clerks	2 clerks
Cost	$30,000	$20,000
Wait time average	10 minutes	9.9 minutes

In every aspect of the above example the express lane approach is better. Our express lane may not be *efficient* at the micro level (on occasion our express clerk might have to wait for a customer with the requisite low number of groceries), but the total store is more *effective* using the express lane approach.

A good manager can still have a store that is not effective. If our store is set up according to the crude model, with all clerks doing every job and not minimizing the processing time variability, the store manager can only add or remove clerks. The store manager can only be as effective as the store design.

The store manager should expect that the store has already been well designed and engineered. Our call center managers should expect the same. The call center design must be periodically reevaluated to assure that our engineering design is still adequate for the policy vision.

Engineering provides the strategic facility that matches the policy vision. Operations must provide a competent workforce to brilliantly execute the plan. To run an effective operation the managers must trust the strategic engineers to have done their job well.

In the 1910s when the first call centers were built all operators did the exact same routing task, and all calls were about the same duration. Call variation stayed a non-issue for decades, and the need for factoring was minimal. With the advent of modern centers with multiple tasks, call processing time variation became a major issue. Today we have the five call center types—routing, notification, call management, processing, and content dissemination. Factoring allows us to identify candidates for express lanes. These call center express lanes keep wait times down, reduce cost, and provide better performance in our responses to customers or users.

The following graph shows us wait time results. The horizontal axis of the graph shows utilizations from 0% to 100%. The vertical axis shows calculated wait time from 0 minutes to 350 minutes. All the line graphs shown have an average processing time of three minutes.

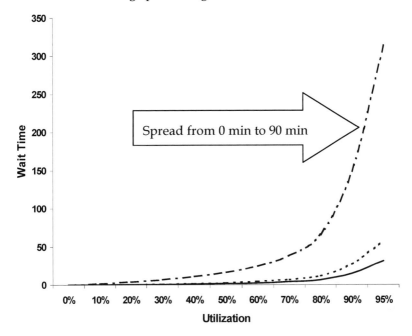

The first graph curve has a call processing time variation from two minutes to four minutes. The spread is relatively small. The wait time curve stays very close to zero and only begins to rise as we approach 90+% utilization. With most calls being close to the average, our wait times are low and manageable.

The second curve is the dashed line. It represents the change in processing time variability from call to call. This call-to-call processing time variation produces a larger spread. The call processing time variation for one call may go as high as 15 minutes and then drop to zero minutes. As the spread from call to call increases, the wait times begin to grow past 70% utilization. Comparing the first curve with minimal call processing time variation, to the second situation with higher variation, we see that we must have lower utilizations to keep the comparable wait times of the low variation.

A third curve has a very wide spread between calls. The call processing time for an individual call will be somewhere between the zero minute and 90 minute spread. As the spread from call to call processing time increases, the wait times begin to grow past 30% utilization, and the curve shows wait times increasing rapidly.

Comparing the first curve with minimal call processing time variation to the second situation with moderate variation, we see that we must have lower utilizations to keep the comparable wait times of the low variation. When we include high variation the agent utilization must be low.

Call Processing: 3 minutes			
Call Variation	Low	Moderate	High
Agent Utilization	80%	60%	20%
Caller Wait Time	4 minute	4 minute	4 minute

The table above shows a comparison of variations and their impact on wait time, agent utilization, and cost. Factoring is now used to determine the express lane candidates so that we can minimize our variability.

Factoring the Operation and Business

Factoring is *the segmenting of every aspect of the business or operation for the ease of doing business.* The ease is for the user, the agents, and the operation. Factoring is the simplification of complex combinations. This simplification is accomplished by multi-factored analysis of factors and levels. Factoring is the term for this business segmentation. Some examples of the factors that are included in a factoring effort include: customers, business, operation, products, processes, processing time, duration, skill, utilization, users, contact method, content, value, and exposure.

Segmentation can be broken into three homogeneous grouping types:

- Physical
- Associational
- Time-series

Physical groups are *those groups that are physically of like kind.* **Associational Groups** are *physically the same but form groups because the analytical numbers are different.* **Time-series groups** are *from groups over time.*

Homogeneous groups may seem obvious to one person and not to another. Thus clear guidelines are required. Control is another way of saying homogeneous or consistent. We must never allow a mixture of non-homogeneous groups. We cannot mix size 12 and size 9 shoes together in a homogeneous group. Neither can we mix blue shirts with white shirts. An average of a size 10½ shoe or a pale blue shirt would be misleading. Instead, simple common sense is required to properly prepare homogeneous groups. It appears to be obvious to keep groups separate, but this is not always the case. Grouping requirements may be difficult to conceptualize and even harder to assure.

It is critical to properly structure the operation segmentation of your enterprise. This segmentation will include the complete business, operation, products, process, processing time, revenue, cost, customers, agent skills, users, content, and exposure to include just a few.

There are both physical and associational groups. These are the hardest to conceptualize. Machines that are similar, one machine running at ten percent defect versus another machine running at zero percent defect, are physically the same but associationally different. Agents processing calls may physically be the same but associationally different. An agent example could be airline reservations, hotel resort reservations, or IT help desks. Don't confuse associational grouping with skill-based routing where the tasks are different. These examples are for the same skill and process (think regular and express grocery store checkout lanes) but the metrics are different. Once a group is identified, the challenge is understanding why it has occurred.

Association is another way of saying that we only group those things of like kind. These groups are then called homogeneous. Non-homogeneous items must never be placed in the same group.

119

This classification and grouping is designed to organize and simplify. Our center's services are classified for many reasons like:

- Organize and simplify the center
- Operational metrics
- Operational decision-making
- Candidates for express lanes
- Systemic analysis
- Elegantly simple routing

Factoring allows for the segmenting of the business to simplify work, information, and processes, determining express lane candidates, reducing cost, and having an effective operation. Factoring is to identify things of like kind and compile them into factors and levels. Factors are segments. Levels are the groups within the segment.

Factoring Example

Now let's start with an example of an IT service support center. The example center uses a universal agent approach where all agents take any and all types of calls. These calls range from the very simple to the extremely complex. These calls also range from the short to the very long. This has driven the variability up in every aspect of the IT operation.

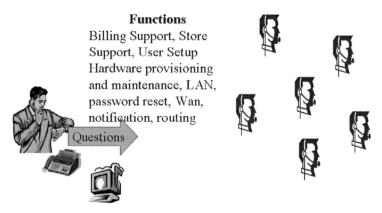

Functions
Billing Support, Store Support, User Setup Hardware provisioning and maintenance, LAN, password reset, Wan, notification, routing

Questions

Segmentation requires analysis of the existing business and operational information. The IT service support center example gives us a chance to see this analysis. The available ticket information from the support center is analyzed for all work within the last period. This ticketing system information must be both accurate and properly prepared. For the analysis the system must have effective coding, time stamps, disposition, and causes. The time stamps must include the creation date, closure date, completion date, duration times, work time, etc. Any comment fields will need to be converted into a structured file format. Without this structure no analysis will be effective.

Next, a list of all supported technology is established. This list is basic services, applications supported, and assets. Any available resource, such as accounting fixed asset or ITIL asset inventories, is a vital piece of information. Common issues like connectivity, authentication, configuration, loading, and systems availability are researched for segmentation.

The IT technology is segmented. This segmentation can start with the office technology like projectors, scanners, copiers, faxes, printers and other common office productivity tools. These office technologies are analyzed for segmentation potential. Common issues, like provisioning, deployment, and redeployment, are identified and then segmented. The asset reference manuals, purchasing documentation, warranties, and repair, are also segmented.

The number and type of system users must also be analyzed. These are analyzed for who is authorized to call for support, VIP issues, usage patterns, and user skills. The users are also segmented into levels like novice, intermediate, advanced, and expert.

Any available IT operational performance monitoring, like bandwidth monitoring, is analyzed for segments. Finally, local subject matter experts (SME) are interviewed for information. They can provide a vital clarification of missing data and resolution of any ambiguities in source documents.

The analysis of the center metrics (like call volume, time of day loads, processing time, wait time, causal information, load peaks and valleys, etc.) uses the techniques of multi-factored analysis of variance, mean testing, and variance testing. This analysis is based on the statistical analysis of mean testing, variance testing, and ANOVA. This approach can determine associational differences for factors and levels and is called mean testing or confidence interval analysis.

Segmentation Uses

At one time or another most people have called a support center or help desk, and they know that the better ones make a record of each customer contact in a ticketing system. Tickets are more than automated "called while you were out" systems. A ticketing system is a communication, tracking, and inventory system. The ticketing system must be built to support an integrated help desk design and operation. A factored help desk achieves an elegantly smooth environment, which is a prerequisite for a ticketing system supporting an effective operation.

Ticket System Design

The ticket design needs to be created in coordination with the operational design for the service business, and modified when the business changes. The heart of the ticket design is the factored, segmented classifications that organize and simplify.

Well-designed classification systems allow a service tech to classify a ticket into one of a thousand categories with the help of well organized and simplified selections. This makes much more sense than searching through a master list of thousands of request types. The design should recognize that, at first contact, there may not be enough information for a complete ticket classification. This classification system should drive the request for service into standardized processes and template solutions.

Metrics

Another area where segmentation is critical is metrics. Poor classification coding can undermine metrics. When you look at tickets from badly designed classification systems, you will typically see a conceptually unusable hodge-podge of symptoms, diagnoses, prescribed solutions, prognoses, and follow-up. Good classification ticket design is difficult.

Perspectives on ticket classification change throughout its life cycle. What starts as a call for email assistance actually becomes an antivirus or network issue. Agents all too often will second guess themselves or make too much use of the other, miscellaneous, or user error codes.

Training

Organizations fighting poor segmentation can find themselves putting agents through months of training before they have confidence that the individual can answer the phone and screen a call. Then after all that time and energy, management finds the agents in a panic and still lacking the skill to accomplish the job at hand.

A properly organized classification system should reflect the business design. The simplified design will allow the rapid deployment of a new hire that is competent to handle the calls in a professional and knowledgeable fashion. A properly factored and deployed system will allow the center to quickly and fairly assess the agents' skill and knowledge.

Express Lane Candidates

After this first round of analysis, lane candidates begin to fall into place. The IT example is segmented into the following areas through factoring: user security, billing support, complex issues, hardware provisioning, notification, routing, hardware maintenance, point of sale store software, LAN/WAN, password reset, and external issues. These groups become our lowest level. In an actual help desk, support center, or call center the number of groups and levels would be much greater, which would radically simplify the operation.

Ordering

To continue our IT example, the next step in our factoring effort is ordering our segments from simple to complex. The following shows our IT service support operation sequentially ranked in order of complexity:

- Routing
- Notification
- Password reset
- User Security
- Billing Support
- POS

- Hardware provisioning
- Hardware Maintenance
- LAN/WAN
- Complex issues
- External

Grouping

Once our factors are identified, determining groupings and items of like kind is our next step. This analysis is based on queuing science and applies logical grouping, staffing, the staff skill sets, and statistical analysis like mean testing, variance testing, and ANOVA.

As an example, let's walk through the math of one of the grouping approaches. This is the same approach used to identify factors and levels. This approach can determine associational groupings and is called mean testing or confidence interval analysis.

The following table shows the results of the confidence interval calculation for each level.

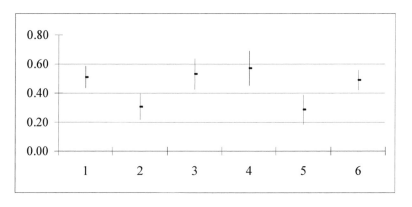

The confidence intervals are plotted on the graph above. We can see that items 1, 3, 4, and 6 form a group,

From this analysis routing, notification, password reset, and user security could be a candidate to form a group. Other possible candidates for grouping could be billing support and POS support. A final group could be formed that contained hardware provisioning, hardware maintenance, LAN/WAN, and complex issues. These grouping candidates do not require a group but form the basis for express lane construction.

Lane Construction

Once groups are established for our current state, lane construction can begin. First the triage group is formed to perform routing and notification.

Next, areas are formed to accomplish the functions of password reset and user security. Then group one is formed for content dissemination for billing support and point of software support.

Finally group two is formed to process requests. These requests include the functions of hardware provisioning, hardware maintenance, LAN/WAN issues, and any other complex issues.

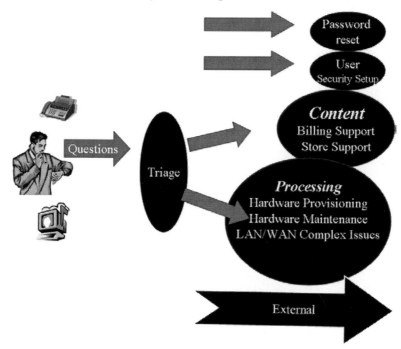

Care must be taken to retain the original segmentation so that grouping and splits can be made when the operation changes.

Staffing the Lanes

Once we've determined our lanes, we can staff based on call volume. Now we have a scientifically engineered center. This center has the requirements for each job area and the area's required skills. Since our center is factored, the metrics can establish load, volume, and processing time so that each area can be staffed appropriately. The chart below shows the express lane staffing for our example.

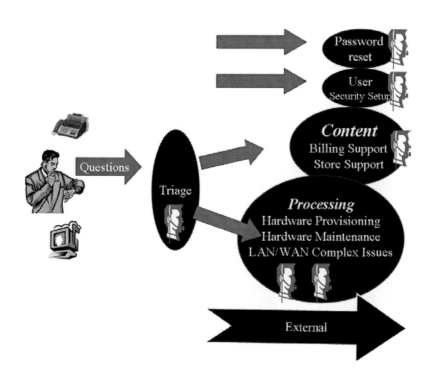

Change

Over time changes will occur to our business. As these changes occur, our center must be optimized so that we always have an effective center design. We must keep our knowledge of lane candidates for grouping and splits, deploying agents, redeployment of staff, and realigning the groupings.

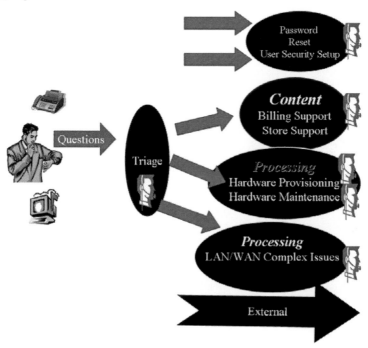

Care must be taken to view our knowledge of segmentation as a company asset. We must guard against ever losing our segmentation knowledge. We must also guard against complacency that we have the ultimate segmentation solution. Finally, we must revisit the factoring effort periodically to assure that we have the best design possible.

Comparison

The benefits associated with a well-engineered contact or service center operation are shorter wait times, better customer satisfaction, targeted SLAs, better utilization, lower cost, better performance, redeployment strategies, happier staff, better coefficient of value, and clarity of what the operations team can do. The advantages of the sigma-designed center versus the pooled approach should now be clear.

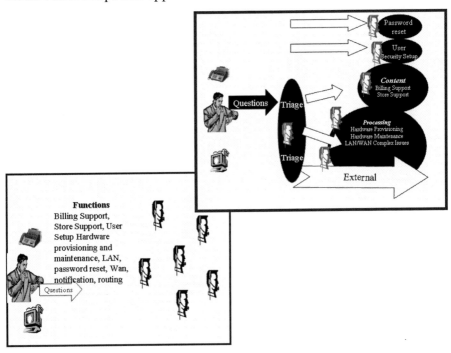

Chapter Ten:
Coefficient of Value

Wait time is a function of processing time average, processing time variability, and agent utilization. Average monitors the central tendency, and standard deviation monitors the variability. The chart below shows an average processing time of three minutes and associated sigma monitored by standard deviations. One standard deviation is small and the other is larger.

Note that 99.8% of calls with the low variation of 0.3 minutes will fall between two and four minutes processing time. The range is derived from a probability calculation. It is important to understand the spread of the calls and their impact on wait time.

The range of 99.8% of the calls with the larger variation of 3.0 minutes will fall between zero and 15 minutes processing time. This spread will have a large wait time if all the other drivers are kept stable.

The third standard deviation of 30 minutes is a large amount of variability for an average processing time of three minutes. This larger spread will have between zero and 90 minutes processing time for 99.8% of calls. This spread will have a longer wait time if all the other drivers are kept stable.

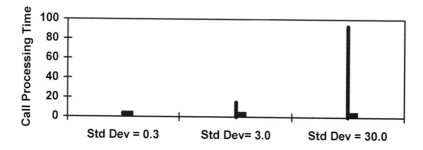

Average Call Processing Time of 3 minutes

The following is a simple example of the variability's impact on wait time. The following graph shows calls arriving every three minutes.

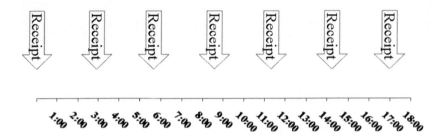

The next graph now adds a processing time of three minutes.

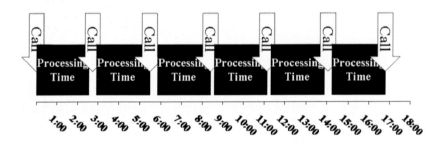

These show a perfectly balanced system that has no wait time. Since we don't live in a perfect world, let's add some complexity into our example by introducing some variability of the processing time.

Variation's Impact on Wait Time

The receipt time will still be three minutes with an average processing time of three minutes. The new twist will be every other call will change in length of processing times. The first call will be five minutes, the second call one minute, and so on. Our average processing time is still three minutes, but we have introduced variability into the processing time.

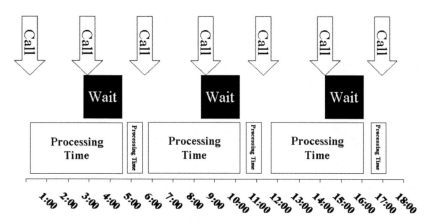

Note how the wait time has jumped. The more variation we add to the driver of processing time the higher the wait time. Many people will ask how is it possible to have wait time when we have idle capacity or agents.

Variation's Impact on Utilization

Now let's slightly change our example. The receipt time will still be three minutes with an average processing time of 2.5 minutes. The new twist will be every other call will change in processing times. The first call will be four minutes, the second call one minute, and so on. Our average processing time is now 2.5 minutes but now we have an agent utilization of 83%.

The chart below shows this example with an agent utilization of 83% and that we have both agents with idle time and callers who wait.

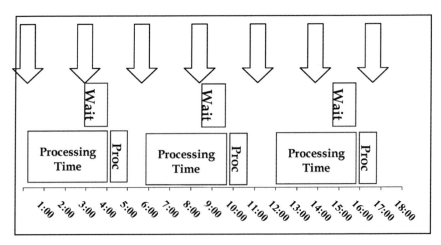

The equation that computes wait time from these three — processing time, utilization, and processing time sigma or variability — is called Pollaczek-Kyntchin equation. For the details of queuing science and Pollaczek-Kyntchin equation read *Designing Effective Call Centers*.

Using the wait time equation we can compute wait time. The example has a scenario with an average processing time of 3.0 minutes and a low sigma of .3 minutes. So we can insert into the equation the processing time monitored with $\mu=3.0$ minutes and a sigma=0.3 minutes are calculated. The agent utilization is equal to ten percent. These are inserted into the wait time equation below and a user wait time of .2 minutes is determined.

Now we can continue the calculations for 20%, 30%, 40%, etc. till we reach 95%. The results of those calculations are shown in the table below:

Utili-za-tion	0%	10%	20%	30%	40%	50%	60%	70%	80%	90%	95%
Wait Time	0.0	0.2	0.4	0.7	1.1	1.7	2.5	3.9	6.6	14.9	31.4

These wait times allow us to construct the wait time curve below:

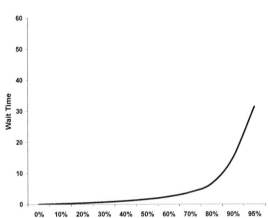

Variability and Cost

To continue our example, let's see the cost of our center and the impact variation has on our cost. Using the same processing time average of three minutes and standard deviation of .3 minutes, we can calculate that a seven-minute wait is reached when the utilization is at 81%.

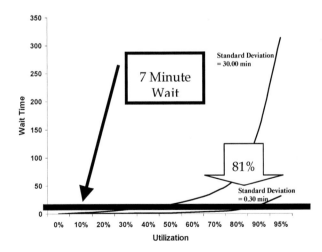

We can obtain some new information from our center. The first thing is the call center call volume of 98,000 calls. The second thing is the agent cost of $20 per hour. We also learn the processing time average of $\mu = 3.0$ minutes and the variation of $\sigma = 0.3$ minutes. These values can be inserted into the equation below to calculate a monthly center cost for the agent of $119,778.

$$\text{Total Cost} = ((\mu * volume)/Util) * Rate$$
$$= ((3.0 * 98,000)/81\%) * (($20/hour)/60\,min/hour)$$
$$= (294,000\,min/.81) * \$.33/min$$
$$= 362963\,min * \$.33/min$$
$$= \$119778$$

Let's continue the example except we'll change one component. We will change the processing time variability to an s = 3.0 minutes. From this change we can see that a seven-minute wait is achieved when the utilization is at 70%.

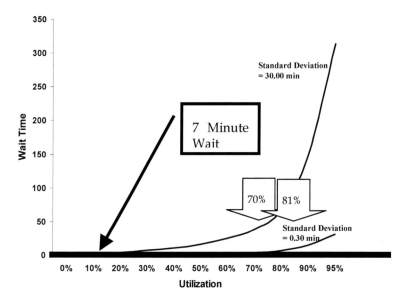

This one change of increased variability calculates a monthly center cost for the agent of $139,860.

$$\text{Total Cost} = ((\mu * volume) / Util) * Rate$$
$$= ((3.0 * 98,000) / 70\%) * (($20 / hour) / 60\,min/ hour)$$
$$= (294,000\,min/ .70) * \$.33 / min$$
$$= 294,000\,min * \$.33 / min$$
$$= \$139860$$

The table below shows the cost differences that reduced variation would achieve. The savings from the variation of 0.3 minute to a variation of 3.0 minutes is the center cost difference of $139,860 minus $119,778 equaling a savings of $20,082.

Standard Deviation	Utilization	Cost
0.3 minutes	81%	$119,778
3.0 minutes	70%	$139,860

Now let's do the same analysis for a very large sigma of 30.0 minutes. This change has a huge impact—to keep the wait time at seven minutes a utilization of 30% is now required.

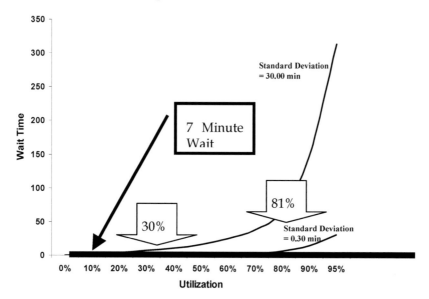

This one change dramatically increases the monthly center cost to $326,340 because of the low (30%) utilization.

The table below shows the cost of the three scenarios and the resultant savings that can be achieved by managing variability. When we design for minimal variability, we will dramatically reduce cost while improving the customer experience. The express lane concept is justified by the potential savings of over $206,000.

Standard Deviation	Utilization	Cost	Savings
0.3 minutes	81%	$119,778	$20,082
3.0 minutes	70%	$139,860	$186,480
30.0 minutes	30%	$326,340	

Our sigma design and variability management are built to reduce cost and keep our center efficient. Thanks to our sigma design we can reduce the sigma from 30.0 minutes to 0.3 minutes, giving us the potential to reduce our cost by over $206,000. Achieving the savings will surely require an investment in knowledgeable design resources, technology, and metrics. Even with this investment, the ROI (return on investment) will be large.

Now to round out and balance the effort, let's see how we can use this knowledge to add the customer to our equation and compute the coefficient of value.

Balance

Our focus so far has been to understand what the driving issues of wait time are. Now it is obvious that this is a multidimensional problem. We need to extend our study of this problem, but we need to exercise care that our focus is not just on keeping the internal cost low.

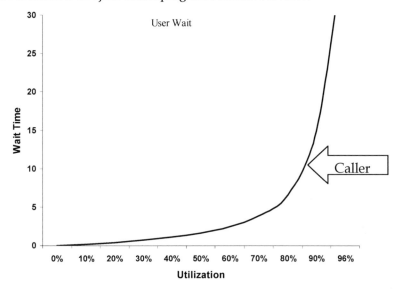

So far our efforts really haven't built on an effectively balanced center. Now we need to build a strategy for an effective operation that balances our user and our internal cost.

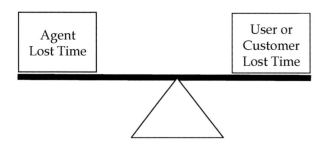

We need to add to our customer wait time curve. The customer wait time curve is really customer or user lost time. We need to balance our agent idle time (lost time) and the user/customer lost time. Then we work to balance and achieve an effective operation.

The curve below shows our agents as their utilization drops. As the utilization drops, their available time increases. This available time is really lost time to the center. As the utilization decreases the agent lost time increases.

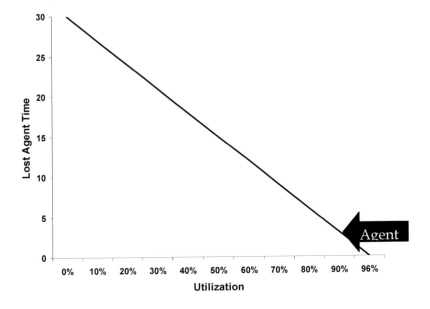

Now we place both the agent lost time curve and the customer lost time curve on the same graph. We see where the two curves cross. We also see that the two are working at cross or opposing purposes.

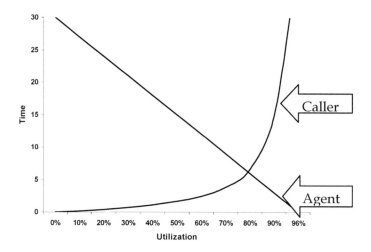

To get the total center picture we can add the agent lost time and customer lost time and the result is the total lost time curve below.

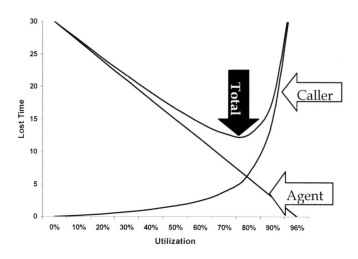

139

To simplify the graph we have removed the detail curves leaving only total lost time. Viewing just the total lost time allows us to see the spot at which the total lost time is at its lowest point. This low value is where the optimum lost time would be when the balance of agent lost time and customer lost time are at their lowest.

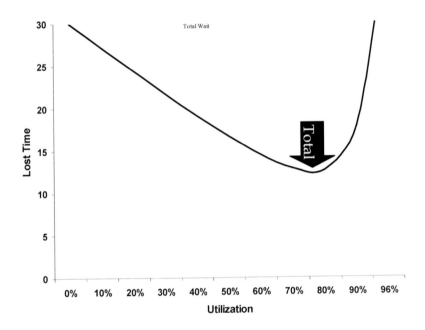

Usually the agent's time and the customer's time are not of equal value. Take the situation where a surgeon who is in the middle of surgery is calling an IT helpdesk to ask a question about the technology used during surgery. Who is more important—the agent or the surgeon? Whose time is more important—the agent's or the surgeon's? This question does not imply that the agent is not important but that we must establish a method to give weight to each component.

A simple way to establish a balance is to determine a monetary value for each component. The monetary weight can either be an actual cost or a weighting factor. We will refer to this new balanced analysis as the **Coefficient of Value.**

Coefficient of Value

We will apply a dollar value to the agent and customer lost time curves. For our first example we will have the agent and customer with equal value. The user's (customer's) value is $20 per hour and the agent's value is $20 per hour. The $20 agent rate is multiplied times the agent lost time for each spot on the lost time curve. The $20 customer value per hour is multiplied times the customer lost time for each spot on the lost wait time curve. The graphs are then redrawn. Finally, the agent curve and the customer curve are added together to establish the lost time cost curve. Where the curve is at its lowest is the optimum spot for this center scenario.

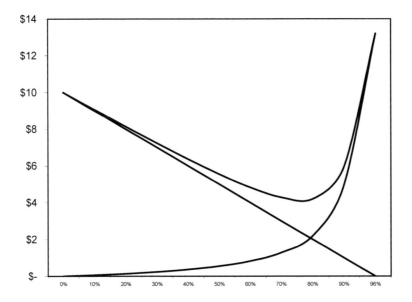

The minimum lost time cost is about $5 per call. This balances our two issues and establishes the minimum cost per call and the optimum utilization for the center where weight is given to both customers' lost time and agents' lost time.

Let's see the impact of changing the customer's value to $60 per hour while the agent's value stays at the original $20 per hour.

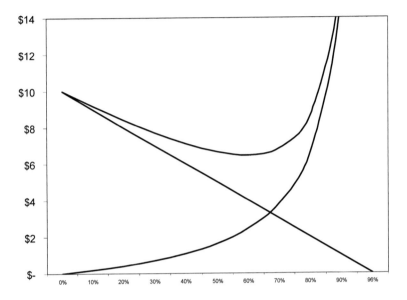

When we redraw the curves the cost rises to close to $8 per call, but notice that the optimum utilization has dropped from 85% to about 65%. This allows us to establish an optimum based on the dynamics of both our center and our customers.

When we compare the two total lost time cost curves on one graph, it is easy to see the impact of how the extra weight of the increased customer's value shifts our optimum agent utilization. The agent's utilization must be reduced to keep a balance in the center. We strategically decide to balance our center by using lower utilizations.

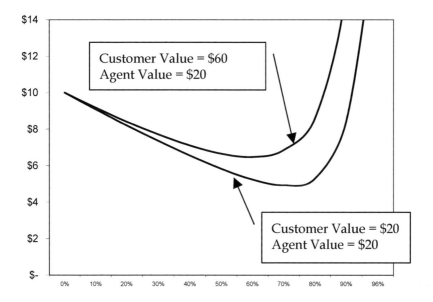

Now we return to our original scenario of a customer value of $20 per hour and an agent value of $20 per hour. Using those costs let's compare sigma values with variabilities of 0.3 minutes, 3.0 minutes, 6.0 minutes, and 30.0 minutes. The four charts are shown below.

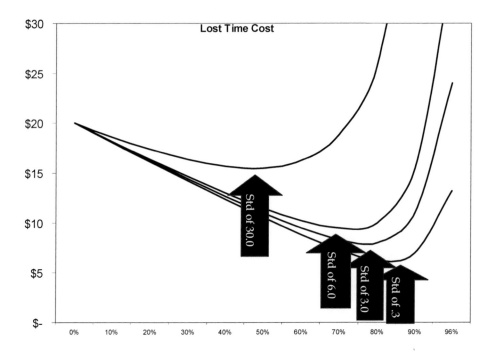

The table below shows the optimum utilization and the minimum lost opportunity cost for increasing sigma monitored by standard deviation.

Standard Deviation	Optimum Utilization	Minimum Lost Time Cost per Call
0.3	85%	$6.12
3.0	76%	$7.97
6.0	72%	$9.47
30.0	47%	$15.48

With this data we can compute total center lost time cost. The processing time average equals 3.0 minutes with a sigma equal to 0.3 minutes. At the optimum utilization of 85% our lost time cost per call is $6.12. With a call volume of 98,000 calls we can use the following equation to calculate total monthly and annual lost time cost.

$$\text{Lost Opportunity Cost} = (\$/call_{Std}) * \text{Call Volume}$$

We can insert our known information into the equation and then compute the monthly and annual cost.

$$\text{Lost Opportunity Cost} = (\$/call_{Std}) * \text{Call Volume}$$
$$= (\$6.12_{Std=0.3}) * 98000 calls$$
$$= \$599,760 / month$$
$$or \ \$7,197,120/year$$

Now we change our scenario to a customer value of $60 per hour and keep all the other constraints the same. An agent's value is $20 per hour. Using those costs let's compare with variability sigma values of 0.3 minutes, 3.0 minutes, 6.0 minutes, and 30.0 minutes.

Standard Deviation	Optimum Utilization	Minimum Lost time Cost per Call
0.3	72%	$9.84
3.0	61%	$12.49
6.0	53%	$14.47
30.0	10%	$19.83

The four charts are shown below. Note how the curves shift to reduce utilization causing an increase in lost time cost.

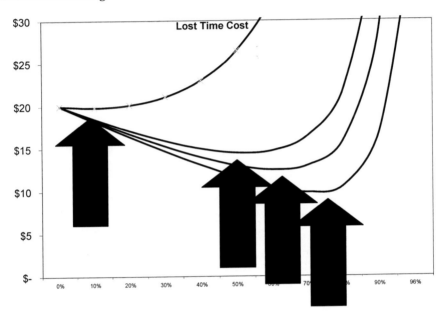

The table below shows the comparison of the lost time opportunity cost for the two scenarios. The first scenario is with the user value of $20 per hour and the agent value of $20 per hour. The second scenario is with the user value of $60 per hour and the agent value of $20 per hour.

Lost Time Opportunity Cost per Call		
Standard Deviation	User =$20 Agent=$20	User =$60 Agent =$20
0.3	$6.12	$9.84
3.0	$7.97	$12.49
6.0	$9.47	$14.47
30.0	15.48	$19.83

The same total lost time cost formula used earlier can also be used with a customer value of $60 and an agent value of $20. This is now included with monthly call volume of 98,000 calls to compute a total lost opportunity cost of $1,240,000 per month or an annual total cost of $14,688,000.

$$\text{Cost} = (\$/call_{Std}) * \text{Call Volume}$$
$$= (\$12.49_{Std=3.0}) * 98000 calls$$
$$= \$1,240,020/month$$

$$= \$14,688,240/year$$

This calculation can be done for every combination to see the total lost cost.

The lost time opportunity cost savings through a variation reduction sigma project can now be calculated. This comparison is based on the user value of $60 per hour and the agent value of $20 per hour.

When the sigma is monitored with a standard deviation of 3.0 minutes, the minimum lost time opportunity cost is $12.49. Compare this to the minimum lost time opportunity cost of $9.84 when the sigma is monitored with a standard deviation of 0.3 minutes.

$$\text{Cost Savings} = (\$/call_{Std} - \$/call_{Std}) * \text{Call Volume}$$
$$= (\$12.49_{Std=3.0} - \$9.84_{Std=.3}) * 98000 calls$$
$$= (\$2.65/call) * 98000 calls$$
$$= \$259,700/month$$

$$= \$3,116,400/year$$

To compute a return through a variation reduction, we compare the savings of $259,700 per month to the total monthly cost per month of $1,240,020.

$$\% \text{ Improve} = (\text{Savings}_{\text{from Variation Reduction}} / \text{ Total Lost Time in \$}) * 100\%$$

$$=$$

$$= (\$259,700 / \$1,240,020) * 100\%$$

$$= 20.9\%$$

This shows a return of over 20%.

Now our final scenario compares a customer value to $10 per hour and we keep all the other constraints the same. An agent's value is $20 per hour. Using those cost now lets compare with the same variability sigma values of 0.3 minutes, 3.0 minutes, 6.0 minutes, and 30.0 minutes. The four charts are shown below.

This scenario allows us to compare a situation where the user's value is less than the center or agents' value

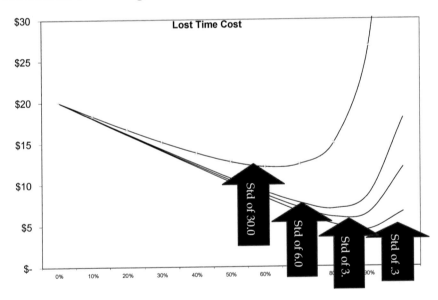

This chart allows us to see that the agent utilizations shift to the right side of the utilization axis with much larger utilizations being the minimum lost time. This minimum is the optimum when we give more value to our center rather than to the customer or user.

Summary

In every business or operation there is a science that must be applied. In an electric motor plant we would apply electrical and mechanical science. In a petrochemical plant we must understand and apply chemistry. In the call center and help desk world we must understand and apply queuing science. The lost time curves give us the ability to apply queuing science to all our process designs and method selections.

User Value of $60 per hour and Agent Value of $20 per hour

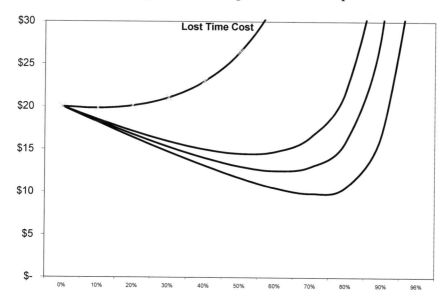

Optimizing a Sigma Design

Hopefully by now the idea of simply using an average seems more than crude. It is so old school! With the rapid and dynamically changing world we live in variability is not an option. Variability must be understood, designed for, and managed.

Note the two graphs that follow both have an average of 30 minutes. The first graph has a large variation while the second graph has a small variation. With this knowledge we can improve the engineering design of our call center. All tactical and strategic decision-makers must appreciate the importance of variability on this metric, plus this metric's affect on other metrics.

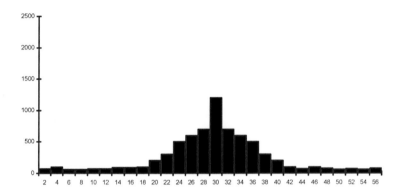

In our old world we could manage using only averages because the variability was always small, not by design, but because we lived in a simpler time. We could staff to an average and ignore variability, and still be okay because the simpler world had virtually no variability.

Now the world has changed and large variability is our starting point. If we use our past techniques and ignore the large variability we will pay a dear price by alienating our customers, our stockholders, and our employees.

Large variation is our starting point, but we do not have to just sit back and ignore it. We must engineer our process, products, and services to minimize variability.

When the variability is included in the engineering equation, we can minimize the variability like the example below.

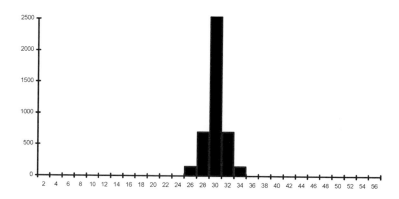

With the smaller variability, if the strategist decides to add additional information into the script, then we will not exceed the SLA. If the SLA is reduced (e.g. SLA = 40 minutes) the first scenario is in trouble, while this scenario would still be very capable.

This is just a few of the many strategic options that are available when we engineer, manage, and keep our variability low. With the first graph of high variability, there are no options available to the strategist. This reinforces the need to communicate to our entire tactical workforce-- both supervisors and agents—the importance of following the plan. This is similar to the express lane grocery store clerk not having people with more than ten items in their lane. Brilliant tactical execution is vital to the effective operation of a call center.

Our grocery store checkout example showed the impact of the driving factors on wait time. Just as in the grocery store, call center wait time is a function of utilization of the agent or rep, processing time average, and the processing time variability. In the grocery store and a call center, short waits don't just happen. We must design the center and then manage the center to obtain the desired results. The express lanes are a function of the driving factors and a scientific design.

Now we can use science, metrics, and statistics and then decide on a risk to make facility determinations. Examples of these, to name a few, are:

- Staffing
- Call volume
- Utilization
- Backlog of open calls

To staff our facility based on call processing time could enhance our center. In years past we staffed to the average processing time and this worked well for us as long as the variability was small. In today's modern center variability is a very real issue. Using the past practice of average processing time as our staffing base line, our center is under-staffed half the time. The magnitude of this understaffing is directly related to the magnitude of the variability. To include variability in these projections, we must make a strategic decision as to how much risk we are prepared to take of not having enough agents.

The following shows us how to reverse the metric process to calculate things like staffing.

Risk Management

We make decisions on information we've prepared as well as we can, but there's always a chance that our information is flawed. For our purposes here, risk management is the risk that our decision-making information is flawed. The following shows the formula adjustments required.

The English literature class where the teacher graded on a normal or bell-shaped curve is an example of having known probabilities and arriving at the number of occurrences or the particular spot. The Z-value formula below allows us to calculate those spots.

$$Z = \left| \frac{X_{Ave} - X_i}{Std} \right|$$

Now the equation is rearranged using algebra to solve for X_i. The resulting equation — called prediction intervals — becomes:

$$X_i = X_{Ave} \pm Z * Std$$

Our strategic decision-maker decides that we will take a 5% risk of a call taking longer than the computed (X_i) time to process. This risk allows us to determine a corresponding Z.

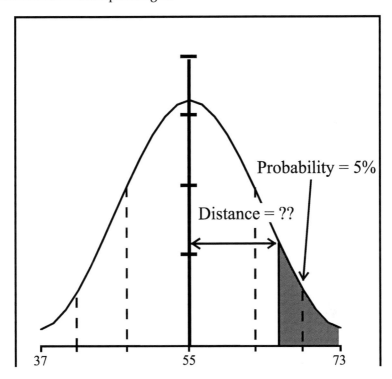

The 5% is converted to .05 probabilities or 5 out of a 100 occurrences of our information being flawed. When converting from a percentage to a Z, we use a normal distribution table. If you are not familiar with the normal table, you should talk to your metrics analyst.

For our example, compute the pickup time range where 90% of the pickup times fall inside this calculated range. Stated another way, calculate the risk of 5% being above the upper range point and the risk that 5% are below the lower calculated point.

First, the Z associated with 5% risk must be determined. Five percent equates to .05. Now we go to the normal table and look in the body for the value closest to .05. The Z of 1.64 and 1.65 or 1.645 is selected.

The average call processing time is 55 seconds and the standard deviation of the processing time is 6 seconds. Both the average and standard deviation are used in conjunction with the selected Z of 1.645 to compute the selected spots. We use the following equation to compute X_i:

$$X_i = X_{Ave} \pm Z * Std$$

In this equation we insert the call processing time average of 55 seconds and the standard deviation of 6 seconds. Now we insert the Z of 5% into the equation. The equation has a Z of 1.645 inserted.

$$X_i = 55 \pm 1.645 * 6$$

Solving the multiplication, the equation now reads:

$$X_i = 55 \pm 9.87$$

Finally,

$$X_i = 45.13 \longleftrightarrow 64.87$$

Thus, 5% of the calls should have a processing time above 64.87 seconds and 5% of the calls should have a processing time under 45.13 seconds. Ninety percent of the calls should be inside the range of 45.13 to 64.87 seconds to process. In the context of our example the 64.87 seconds processing time is the most meaningful and would be used for staffing.

Risk Management Table

Expanding the prediction area we can build a risk management table that will show spots where our call center metrics will fall. The strategic decision-makers use the table below after they have selected the appropriate risk for the metric under study. The first column is the percentage risk we are prepared to take that our metric under study will exceed a spot. The second column is the percentage converted into the number of occurrences that that will exceed out of a total. The final column is the Z factor that the strategist will use in calculations for establishing optimum center levels.

Risk Management Table		
% Risk of Exceeding	# of Occurrences Exceeding	Z
50%	1 out of 2	0
30%	3 out of 10	.53
16%	16 out of 100	1
10%	10 out of 100	1.28
5%	5 out of 100	1.645
2.3%	2.3 out of 100	2
.1%	1 out of 1,000	3
.003%	3 out of 100,000	4
.00003%	3 out of 10 million	5
.0000001%	1 out of 1 billion	6

Now we can use the selected risk to make predictions in our call center and support the strategic role of assessing the center capability.

SLAs must be developed for predicting an individual call and its results. Since call center complexity has radically increased, the SLAs must continually be assessed for their accuracy and validity. The days of being able to use a simple average for an SLA passed away in the evolution to five different call center types. In our multifunction centers, variability and distribution are of equal importance to central tendency. To monitor variability and the data distribution, we must have the individual call information to analyze.

With good, well-formed SLAs we can compare what our customer will tolerate to what our center is actually doing. First, we can superimpose the two issues on one histogram. The SLA shows the spot we would declare our service to be totally unacceptable to any one of our customers.

To keep our center running at optimal levels, we will need metric descriptions of central tendency, variability, and distribution. Next our strategist must define the acceptable risk for their center and the study area. With the defined risk and metric description the following equation can be used to make estimates:

$$X_i = X_{Ave} \pm Z*Std$$

Now we have the tools to run and maintain an optimal center. This continual optimization will include the following as examples: staffing, call volume, utilization, backlog of open calls, etc. Now let's do a staffing example.

Staffing

For our staffing example the metrics of call volume, processing time, and utilization must be described and the risk defined. To keep our example simple enough to follow we will fully expand the processing time and assume no variability for the call volume and utilization.

The processing time has an average of five minutes, a standard deviation of 0.5 minutes, and the processing time distribution is normal. The number of calls per day is 115. From our queuing science balancing we have strategically selected a utilization of 73%. We will use all of these in staffing equations.

Our first calculation is the call processing time. The strategist selects and will accept a ten percent risk of not having enough staffing to support our call processing times. From our risk management table a 10% has a corresponding Z value of 1.28. The following equation is used to compute the processing time with a ten percent risk.

$$X_i = X_{Ave} \pm Z * Std_{Ind}$$

Now we insert the processing time average of five minutes and a standard deviation of 0.5 minutes into the equation as shown below.

$$X_i = X_{Ave} \pm Z * Std$$
$$= 5 + 1.28 * .5$$
$$= 5 + .64$$
$$= 5.64 \text{ minutes per call}$$

Next we take the processing time and the call volume of 115 calls per day and compute the total processing time required at full (100%) utilization. These are inserted in the equation below:

$$\text{Total time} = \text{Processing time} * \text{Call Volume}$$
$$= 5.64 \text{ minutes / call} * 115 \text{ calls per day}$$
$$= 648.6 \text{ minutes per day}$$

Next, to determine the required processing time or agent available time, we must factor in the 73% utilization to balance the wait time.

$$\text{Required Available} = (\text{Total Processing Time/utilization})$$
$$= 648.6\text{min} / 73\%$$
$$= 889 \text{ minutes}$$

This calculation shows that we need 889 minutes of available agent time to provide the level of service that our strategist has determined.

Converting the 889 minutes into hours, we find that 14.8 hours of available agent time are required. We will need to compute how many agents will be needed for this number of hours. In our example center the agents work 7.5 hours per day.

$$\text{Staffing} = 14.8hr / 7.5hr$$
$$= 1.97 \text{ or } 2\text{agents}$$

Remember we have assumed no variability for the call volume and utilization for our example. Since you cannot have a partial agent, we must always round up to the next highest whole agent. So for our example, we will need two agents to support the level of service that our strategist has selected.

Six Sigma Design Impact

Now let's see the impact of a scientifically designed six sigma center versus a design that ignores variability or sigma. In the chapter *Sigma Designs in a Call Center,* the National Candy Company IT help desk was our example. This help desk will be the example we use to compare the approaches. This IT help desk supports desktop users, new user setup, finance questions, point of sale software support, and network issues. The five call center areas with their processing time metric descriptions are listed below. For our first analysis, this design has every agent taking every call type. To our table we will add the call volume per day for each call type assuming no variability to simplify the example.

	Call Processing Time in Minutes					
	All Type	Desk-top	New User Setup	Finance	Point of Sale - Product	Net-work
Average	51	19	21	27	30	150
Std Deviation	53	.8	.4	.5	3	35
Call Volume per Day	200	100	25	20	50	5

The all-type average is not close to any single value. Also, the all-type standard deviation of 53 minutes is radically larger than any of the individual groups' standard deviations. The individual area standard deviations are desktop .8 minutes, new user setup .4 minutes, financial support .4 minutes, point of sale product support 3 minutes, and network 35 minutes. The all types approach has an average of 51 minutes and a standard deviation of 53 minutes. If all the agents try to do every type of call we must use these to calculate our wait time, and the waits will be extremely high. We have already seen the impact of high processing time sigma on wait time; let's see the impact on our staffing.

If we staff at the processing time average of 51 minutes, our center will be understaffed fifty percent of the time. We can calculate staffing to the average. The equation for the required processing time is shown below.

When we use the average only we are taking a fifty percent risk and a Z of 0 is used in our equation.

$$X_i = X_{Ave} \pm Z * Std$$
$$= 51 + 0 * 53$$
$$= 51 + 0$$
$$= 51 \text{ minutes per call}$$

Now we insert 51 minutes per call into our total time equation and calculate the required time.

$$\text{Total time} = \text{Processing time} * \text{Call Volume}$$
$$= 51 \text{ minutes} / \text{call} * 200 \text{ calls per day}$$
$$= 10{,}200 \text{ minutes per day}$$

On the surface the 10,200 minutes of required processing time sounds reasonable, but fifty percent of the time we will be understaffed. With a high variability this understaffing will be huge, and it will negatively impact every aspect of the center.

We must reduce our risk, but we will pay a price in required time. The strategist designs to a six sigma level or to a level with virtually no risk. The following equation is used to compute the processing time. Now we insert the processing time average of 51 minutes and a standard deviation of 53 minutes into the equation as shown below.

$$X_i = X_{Ave} \pm Z * Std$$
$$= 51 + 6.00 * 53$$
$$= 51 + 318$$
$$= 369 \text{ minutes per call}$$

Next we take the processing time and the call volume of 200 calls per day and compute the total processing time required at full utilization or 100% utilization. These are inserted in the equation below.

$$\text{Total time} = \text{Processing time} * \text{Call Volume}$$
$$= 369 \text{ minutes} / \text{call} * 200 \text{ calls per day}$$
$$= 73800 \text{ minutes per day}$$

This is a huge price in total minutes. By taking larger risks we can build the following table to show the required minutes.

Risk	Z	Required Minutes
50%	0.00	10,200
30%	0.53	15,818
10%	1.28	23,768
5%	1.645	27,637
Six Sigma Level	6.00	73,800

Notice how quickly the required time jumps as the risk is reduced. Let's compare this to a scientifically designed center.

Now we'll do the same calculation except we'll base it on a six sigma center design with express lanes. We will work through the details of the desktop support express lane. We insert the processing time average of 19 minutes and a standard deviation of 0.8 minutes into the equation as shown below.

$$X_i = X_{Ave} \pm Z * \text{Std}$$
$$= 19 + 6.00 * 0.8$$
$$= 19 + 4.8$$
$$= 23.8 \text{ minutes per call}$$

Next we take the processing time and the desktop support call volume of 100 calls per day and compute the total processing time required at full utilization or 100% utilization. These are inserted in the equation below.

$$\text{Total time} = \text{Processing time} * \text{Call Volume}$$
$$= 23.8 \text{ minutes} / \text{call} * 100 \text{ calls per day}$$
$$= 2380 \text{ minutes per day}$$

Repeating the calculations for each express lane, we compute the required time for each lane.

	Crude	Call Processing Time in Minutes					
		Express lane					
	All Type	Desk-top	New User Setup	Fi-nance	Point of Sale - Product	Net-work	
Average	51	19	21	27	30	150	
Std Deviation	53	.8	.4	.5	3	35	
Call Volume per Day	200	100	25	20	50	5	
Required Time @ 6 Sigma Level	73800	2380	585	600	2400	1800	
Total Minutes	73,800	7,765					

By totaling each express lane we can compute the center total amount of time required, which is 7,765 minutes.

$$\text{Center Total time} = \text{Desktop} + \text{User setup} + \text{Finance} + \text{POS} + \text{Network}$$
$$= 2380 \text{ min } utes + 585 \text{ min } utes + ... + 1800 \text{ min } utes$$
$$= 7765 \text{ minutes per day}$$

Now we must compare the express lane total required minutes of 7,765 to the crude approach requirement of 73,800 minutes. The required minutes and the associated cost savings difference are huge.

You might say the call volume breakdown is impacting the results so to eliminate that issue let's examine two other call volume distributions. The first uses an even call volume of 40 calls per day for each of the five types.

	Call Processing Time in Minutes					
Crude	**Express lane**					
	All Type	Desktop	New User Setup	Finance	Point of Sale - Product	Net-work
Average	51	19	21	27	30	150
Std Deviation	53	.8	.4	.5	3	35
Call Volume per Day	200	40	40	40	40	40
Required Time @ 6 Sigma Level	73800	952	936	1200	1920	14400

The total required for the express lane is 19,408 minutes compared to the crude approach requirement of 73,800 minutes.

The second will compare an exact reversal of call volume putting the bulk of the calls on the longest processing time lane of networking.

	Call Processing Time in Minutes					
Crude		**Express lane**				
	All Type	**Desktop**	**New User Setup**	**Finance**	**Point of Sale - Product**	**Net-work**
Average	51	19	21	27	30	150
Std Deviation	53	.8	.4	.5	3	35
Call Volume per Day	200	5	50	20	25	100
Required Time @ 6 Sigma Level	73800	119	1170	600	1200	36000

The total required for the express lane is 39,089 minutes compared to the crude 73,800 minutes. No matter how we analyze the center, a sigma design in a call center, help desk, or support center will quickly pay for itself. The order of magnitude of improvement by applying sigma designs though express lanes, metrics, and science is huge.

Chapter Twelve:

Call Center Future

With a six sigma design your call center is not in the 1950s anymore. So far in this book we have covered an extensive list of things we can improve. The list of things that you can do with a sigma-designed center is even longer. The ultimate goal of all our efforts can be paraphrased with one word: value. We need to provide value to our customers, our users, our staff, and our stockholders. Value will take many forms and that is the start of our list of more things you can do.

Earlier I discussed the four traits that I have always found in an effective operation. Trait one is the ability to respond to rapid change. Trait two is a factored organizational structure (express lanes) supported by defined processes. Trait three is a competent workforce that brilliantly executes the business plan. Trait four is optimum decision-making based on proper information.

These four traits serve as a great platform to give a partial list of some of the additional things that you can do with a six sigma call center design. Let's take a go at the first trait of ability to respond to change.

Change is the one constant that we can really count on in this 21st century. This change is moving at a lightning speed. New products and services are the direct result of this change, and they too are coming at lightning speed. With a six sigma design in your center, these new products and services can seamlessly and easily blend into the fold for rapid deployment.

Handling Future Change

We started this book with a list of possibilities that a six sigma design could achieve. As we journey into the future of call centers, we can see how difficult change is in a pooled center. In a "pooled" world everybody has be trained on all the products and services (both existing and new). New associates must be trained on all the old products and services and then also trained on the new products and services.

In a sigma-designed center an express lane can be built to compartmentalize the impact on the center. Existing or new hires will staff the new product express lane. The new product express lane staff will only have to be trained and experienced on the new product, because that is what they will be dealing with.

In the chapter on *Optimizing a Sigma Design* we saw what a large difference in the number of required hours a sigma-designed center had versus one that had no thought given to sigma. The sigma center allows you to reduce the number of required hours and, by managing variability, give a better customer experience. In a pooled center where everyone is doing everything, we can set only one utilization target because all the calls, the agents, and the utilizations are pooled. In a sigma-designed center, in addition to minimizing hours, we can set utilizations for each express lane based on the lane-specific drivers so that we refine our center even more.

In a center where everyone is doing everything in a pool, the only adjustment that can be made is adding or removing people. In a sigma-designed center a supervisor or manager can move resources from one express lane to another to maximize the utilization.

Agent's Future

In the third trait we discussed a competent workforce, which must be built and nurtured. In a sigma design, an agent's training is a step at a time. Just in time training allows the agent to be trained on the roles and responsibilities the agent is going to be immediately working on. With a sigma design and stepped training, we build our competent workforce in a reasonable manner. This approach not only builds our competent workforce, but also saves money because we are getting agents proficient faster.

In a sigma design an agent can migrate through the center increasing their knowledge in a stepped fashion. As each step is accomplished, the agent's knowledge increases. The agent's self worth will grow and the agent's value to the company will grow. This gives a way for us to keep a steady stream of increasingly competent people moving through the center. This gives our agents a career migration path through the center.

As our agent's expertise grows, the center can act as a spawning ground for other parts of the company. The sigma-designed center gives the agents a migration path through the center and a career path out of the center. With realistic agent expectations, career migrations, and career paths, our agent attrition can be managed and reduced.

165

Chapter Twelve

Customer's Future

Companies all say that they value their customers. Many times the company does not act as if they value their customer because they waste their customers' time by making them wait on the phone or computer. If companies paid their customers a cost per minute for each time they made them wait, we might view things very differently. By giving a value to both the center and the customer, we can balance all the issues. Our coefficient of value allows the objective balancing of these issues and gives our customers a great experience each and every time.

The sigma-designed center will allow us to reduce cost but still give the customer a great experience. This balanced view of the center will allow us to contribute to increasing the value of the company. A continued effort to improve the customer experience is the future of call centers. The irony is that as that customer experience gets better, cost will continue to go down in a sigma center.

Future Results Through Sigma Design, Science, and Metrics

Call center strategic decision-makers and engineers must use a sigma design approach, metrics, and science to build and manage state of the art call centers. Understanding call center science is vital to an effective call center.

Six sigma designed centers, science, and metrics provide the knowledge to proactively manage the center to avoid problems.

Our six sigma design must provide the facility to support our policy vision. The design steps below are the roadmap to meet that goal.

1. Factor the business for segmentation
2. Establish a dependency diagram
3. Select the appropriate process method
4. Establish metrics and target settings

Each of these steps is of equal importance. Effective operations are engineered based on science and metrics — science for direction and metrics for status and verification. Effective operations have a competent workforce that brilliantly executes the engineered plan. We will audit the center with metrics.

The goal of this book is to provide the sigma design so you can run the center to its maximum potential all the time. All our efforts are marshaled toward reaching that goal. Running each call center with a sigma design, metrics, and science, to its maximum potential, is vital to our effective operation.

The bigger objective is satisfied customers, stockholders, and a happy call center staff. This objective can be defined as delighting our customer with products that meet or exceed their expectations, while reducing our unit cost, and providing better service to our customers the moment they want it. The three components of this bigger objective are providing flawless service and performance, reducing our cost, and minimizing customer wait time. The performance, cost, and time criteria define the bigger objective.

With a scientifically designed six sigma center reaping the results is a reality. Achieving improved performance, reducing cost, and reducing wait times is now possible, and will continue. Using a sigma design as the base, more and better techniques, methods, tools, and engineering makes the future exciting. It is a future that will delight our stockholders, our customers, and our associates.

Index

A

Associational groups 40, 119

Average 12-14, 17, 32-33

C

Call center types 10, 15, 82, 100, 116

Call management center (*see* call center types)

Capability (*see* Third Principle of Process Management)

Capability study 108-109

Central tendency 12

Change management 38, 94, 103-105

Coefficient of Value 140-148

Consistency (*see* Third Principle of Process Management)

Content dissemination center (*see* call center types)

Control charts 106-108

Correctness (*see* Third Principle of Process Management)

Cost (*see also* quality) 28

D

Decision-making (*see* tactical decisions, strategic decisions, policy decisions)

Dependency diagram 66-67, 72-73, 101-102

Division of Labor (*see* Second Principle of Process Management)

Dropped calls (*see* wait time)

E

Effective call center managers (*see* Four traits of effective call center mangers)

Effective operations (*see* Four traits of effective operations)

Efficient vs. effective 27, 37, 116

Express lanes (*see also* segmentation) 27-28, 81

F

Factoring (*see also* segmentation) 118

First Principle of Process Management 64-65, 71, 74

Four traits of effective managers 84, 105

Four traits of effective operations 37, 84, 105, 164-167

Functional groups (*see* segmentation)

G

Sigma 16, 20, 28, 32-36, 130-136

Six sigma 7, 50, 54-55

SLA (*see* Service Level Agreement)

Specification limits (*see* Service Level Agreement)

Staffing 51-52, 126, 152, 156-158

Standard deviation 20, 32

Strategic decisions, strategists 39, 60-63, 86-89, 94-96

System 114

T

Tactical decisions, tactics 74-75, 86-89, 94-96

Third Principle of Process Management 100-103

Time-series groups 40, 119

Training 123

U

Utilization 9, 33

V

Value 8

Variability 16-17, 20, 26, 33, 37, 44-45, 150-151

Variation (*see* sigma)

Vision statement 62

W

Wait time (*see also*, quality) 26-27, 30-31, 33, 77-79, 91-92, 110

Walkabout® Dependency Diagram 73

Walkabout® Method (*see* change management)

Z

Z-value 53-54

More titles for enhanced call center
design and performance

The Executive Guide to Call Center Metrics, $34.95

Find out why this book has been Amazon.com's #1 best-selling call center metrics book for over three years.

Preparing Call Center Metrics, $195.00

This companion to *The Executive Guide to Call Center Metrics* is now available directly to readers. Learn the critical metrics and data preparation methods for your call center or help desk.

Designing Effective Call Centers, $94.95

The definitive guide to designing call centers and help desks from the ground up.

Order from Amazon.com, your favorite local
bookseller, or visit

www.effectivecallcenters.com

More titles for enhanced call center
design and performance

The Executive Guide to Call Center Metrics, $34.95

Find out why this book has been Amazon.com's #1 best-selling call center metrics book for over three years.

Preparing Call Center Metrics, $195.00

This companion to *The Executive Guide to Call Center Metrics* is now available directly to readers. Learn the critical metrics and data preparation methods for your call center or help desk.

Designing Effective Call Centers, $94.95

The definitive guide to designing call centers and help desks from the ground up.

Order from Amazon.com, your favorite local
bookseller, or visit

www.effectivecallcenters.com